Ninja Foodi

2-Basket Air Fryer

Cookbook for Beginners

1800-Day Easy & Creative Ninja Air Fryer Recipes for Novices to
Prepare Nutritionally Balanced Dishes for Whole Family

Katrice Metzler

Table of Contents

Introduction

One of only a few air fryers featuring two cooking zones with a combined capacity of eight quarts is the Ninja Foodi Dual Basket Air Fryer, also known as the Ninja Foodi DZ201. It is a multifunctional kitchen tool that can air fry, broil, roast, bake, dehydrate, and reheat leftovers. The Ninja Double Air Fryer also comes with useful smart features.

With a twin-basket configuration, it boasts the largest cooking capacity. There is no other brand that provides the same feature: nada, nil, zero, zilch.

In addition to the ample cooking space, it has a few useful functions. First, let's look at the Smart Finish setting. When you're cooking two separate dishes, the Smart Finish option comes in handy. When you configure this parameter, they will all end at the same time. Nothing is cosier than an exquisitely warm supper.

On the other hand, there is a shortcut for replicating the setting of one zone to the other if you are making the same dish. It is marketed as "Match Cook." You may simply hit the match cook button to transfer all the settings to the other basket rather than entering the temperature, cooking time, or mode again. When you're preparing a big quantity of fries or chicken wings, this copy-and-paste feature can be useful.

Fundamentals of Ninja Foodi 2-Basket Air Fryer

With so many options available, choosing the type of air fryer you should purchase can be difficult. Nevertheless, I can advise you because of my lengthy and occasionally rocky relationship with them. I adore the concept of a kitchen appliance that uses hot air circulation to quickly cook food to a nice, crisp consistency without the use of the extra oil required for deep frying. I did, however, have an issue. With the exception of the Ninja Foodi 8-quart, 4-in-1 Dual Zone Air Fryer, all of the countertop appliances I purchased let me down despite the fact that most of them function the same. And the purchase is worthwhile.

Features of the Product
• You can prepare two different dishes using two baskets.
• Utilizing Smart Finish and Match Cook, Dual Zone Technology
• Each zone has 6 present cooking functions.
• Air Fry, Air Boil, Roast, Bake, Reheat, Dehydrate all in one
• XL 8-qt. accommodates up to 4 lbs. French fries.
• Each separate cooking area is equipped with a heater and fan.
• Smart Finish synchronises many settings to complete concurrently.
• Crisper plates that are dishwasher safe and have easy-to-clean baskets
• Match Cook copies settings between the two zones.
• wide range of temperatures: 105°F - 450°F

What is Ninja Foodi 2-Basket Air Fryer?

Air fryers have gained popularity because they promise to fry all of our favourite fries, crispy chicken wings, cookies, and more without needing additional fat. However, using these fashionable appliances calls for cooking in smaller quantities so that the food may cook evenly with unrestricted circulation of air all around it. This implies that those who are cooking for a larger family or group of people will need to prepare several batches.

The Ninja Foodi 6-in-1 8-Quart 2-Basket Air Fryer is now available. Dual baskets on this robust device will let you get the most out of air frying. I so made the decision to try it. I made plans to try out new recipes and purchased frozen items that I could air fried.

This fryer may not be what I'd call handsome, but it does have some attractive design features, such as rounded corners, metal trim, and dark grey surfaces that seem subtle and traditional.

The front handles are quite big and easy to hold, which is ideal because food may need to be shaken or stirred somewhat during cooking. They are also the right size and shape to make it simple to remove cooked food from the basket. Given its height, the fryer should be able to slip beneath cabinets and remain on the counter when not in use.

Although the controls are straightforward, there were a few times when I wasn't sure what to do. I could pause the cooking on either side of the fryer using a Start/Pause button, but I preferred to stop the cooking when food on one side was done sooner than I had anticipated. To inform the fryer that the cooking time was up, the Time function was used as the solution. That was effective, although it wasn't immediately clear.

- Sleek style
- Moderately priced
- Using a basket air fryer is simpler than using a pressure cooker air fryer.
- Two baskets for increased capacity (8-qt total)
- Design of the rectangular basket to hold more food
- A dual-zone system
- Game Cook (copy and paste settings across zones)
- With Smart Finish (syncs the cook time mill)
- Wide range of temperatures (105-450°F)
- Air fry, broil, roast, bake, dehydrate, and reheat are six types of cooking.
- Adjustable cooking time and temperature
- Stainless steel components
- 1-year BPA-free warranty

Prior to First Use

1. Take off and throw away all tape, labels, and packaging from the device.
2. Take out all the accessories from the box and carefully read this handbook. To prevent any injuries or property damage, please pay close attention to operational directions, warnings, and crucial protections.
3. After thoroughly rinsing and drying, wash the baskets and crisper plates in hot, soapy water.
4. Only the crisper plates and baskets are put in the dishwasher. NEVER clean the dishwasher's main unit.

How to use it

This Ninja double air fryer does six other tasks in addition to crisping up your french fries with less oil. Additionally, it can roast, bake, dehydrate, broil, and reheat. It can serve as your go-to kitchen tool for making dinner for the family because to its large capacity.

Function Buttons

AIR BROIL: Finish dishes with a crispy crust or melt toppings for the ideal presentation.

AIR FRY: Use the air fryer to add crunch and crispness to your cuisine while using little to no oil.

ROAST: Use the appliance as a roaster oven for tender meats and more.

REHEAT: Warm up your leftovers so they come out crispy.

DEHYDRATE: Dehydrate fruits, vegetables, and meats for wholesome snacking.

BAKE: Make opulent desserts and baked goods.

Activation Buttons

1 regulates the output for the basket on the left.

2 regulates the output for the basket on the right.

TEMP arrows: To change the cook temperature before or while cooking, use the up and down arrows.

TIME arrows: To change the cook time in any function before or during the cook cycle, use the up and down arrows.

SMART FINISH button: Even if the cook times for the two zones are different, the SMART Complete button automatically synchronises the cook times to guarantee that both zones finish at the same time.

MATCH COOK button: Automatically match zone 2 settings to those of zone 1 so that more of the same food can be cooked at once or that different meals can be prepared at the same function, temperature, and time.

START/PAUSE button: Press the START/PAUSE button to begin cooking after deciding on the temperature and the cooking time. Press the START/Halt button after choosing the zone you want to pause, and the cooking will stop.

POWER BUTTON: This switch powers on and off the appliance and halts all cooking operations.

Standby Mode: The device will go into standby mode if the control panel is not used for 10 minutes. The Power button will have a dimmer.

Hold Mode: When the unit is in SMART FINISH mode, the word "Hold" will appear. While the other zone waits for the times to coincide, one zone will be cooking.

Air Broil

With your standard air fryer, it operates in the same manner. The broil mode is your buddy if you want your meal to have a golden brown finish. It's the ideal setting for the Ninja Foodi DZ201 to melt cheese or give your protein a crunchy texture.

Unfortunately, you can only broil in one zone. Both baskets cannot be broiled at the same time. Zone 1 will automatically perform this task, but you can change zones if necessary.

1. Install the crisper plate in the basket, add the ingredients, and then put the basket into the appliance.
2. Zone 1 will be used by default (choose zone 2 to use zone 2 instead). Choose AIR BROIL.
3. To set the preferred temperature, use the TEMP arrows.
4. To set the time in 1-minute increments up to 30 minutes, use the TIME arrows.
5. To start cooking, press the START/PAUSE button.
6. The appliance will beep and the word "End" will show on the display when the cooking is finished.
7. Utilize tongs or utensils with a silicone tip to remove the ingredients.

Air Fry

You will be aware of the Max Crisp feature if you have read my review of the Ninja Air Fryer Max XL. The button isn't present in the Ninja Foodi Dual Basket Air Fryer because it is already a part of the device. The same 105°F to 450°F temperature range applies.

Simply changing the temperature and adding additional time will increase the crispiness of your fries or fried chicken. A separate Max Crisp button is unnecessary.

1. Install the crisper plate in the basket, add the ingredients, and then put the basket into the appliance.
2. Zone 1 will be used by default; to use zone 2, choose zone 2. Choose AIR FRY.
3. To set the preferred temperature, use the TEMP arrows.
4. To set the time in 1-minute increments up to 1 hour, use the TIME arrows.
5. To start cooking, press the START/PAUSE button.
6. The appliance will beep and the word "End" will show on the display when the cooking is finished.
7. Utilize tongs or utensils with a silicone tip to remove the ingredients.

Roast

On one basket, you can roast your protein, and on the other, you can caramelize your carrots or possibly your Brussels sprouts. The benefit of a two-basket air fryer is that.

1. Place the items in the basket, add the crisper plate (if desired), and then put the basket into the unit.
2. The device will automatically enter zone 1 (to use zone 2 instead, select zone 2). Choose ROAST.
3. To set the preferred temperature, use the TEMP arrows.
4. To set the time in 1-minute increments up to 1 hour and in 5-minute increments from 1 to 4 hours, use the TIME arrows.
5. To start cooking, press the START/PAUSE button.
6. The appliance will beep and "End" will show up on the display when cooking is finished.
7. Utilize tongs or utensils with a silicone tip to remove the ingredients.

Bake

The bake function is by no means noteworthy. For example, using a water bath is difficult. In other words, the Ninja Foodi 2-Basket Air Fryer's baking capabilities are fairly constrained.

However, the ability to prepare a dessert in an air fryer is still a plus.

1. Place the items in the basket, add the crisper plate (if desired), and then put the basket into the unit.
2. Zone 1 will be used by default; to use zone 2, choose zone 2. Choose BAKE.
3. To set the preferred temperature, use the TEMP arrows.
4. To set the time in 1-minute increments up to 1 hour and in 5-minute increments from 1 to 4 hours, use the TIME arrows.
5. To start cooking, press the START/PAUSE button.
6. The appliance will beep and "End" will show up on the display when cooking is finished.
7. Utilize tongs or utensils with a silicone tip to remove the ingredients.

Dehydrate

The capacity to dehydrate is good to have even though it cannot take the place of a conventional dehydrator.

In light of this, the dehydrate feature would be a great advantage if you choose to get the multi-layer rack accessory. Foods must be dried for a long period, so it is advisable to use a multi-level platform and dehydrate them in large quantities.

1. Put the ingredients in the basket in a single layer. Then add another layer of ingredients to the crisper plate, which is now installed in the basket on top of the first layer.
2. Zone 1 will be used by default (choose zone 2 to use zone 2 instead). Select DEHYDRATE. The display will show the current temperature by default. To set the preferred temperature, use the TEMP arrows.
3. Set the time in 15-minute intervals between 1 and 12 hours using the TIME arrows.
Click the START/PAUSE button to start the dehydration process.
4. The appliance will beep and the word "End" will show on the display when the cooking is finished.
5. Utilize tongs or utensils with a silicone tip to remove the ingredients.

Reheat

Use the Ninja Foodi Air Fryer to reheat fried dishes rather than a microwave. It will provide a crispier and more flavourful outcome.
For smooth cooking, shake or flip your items using non-abrasive tongs.

1. Place the items in the basket, add the crisper plate (if desired), and then put the basket into the unit.
2. Zone 1 will be used by default; to use zone 2, choose zone 2. Choose REHEAT.
3. To set the preferred temperature, use the TEMP arrows.
4. To set the time in 1-minute increments up to an hour, use the TIME arrows.
5. In order to start warming, use the START/PAUSE button.
6. The device will beep and "End" will show up on the display after warming is finished.
7. Utilize tongs or utensils with a silicone tip to remove the ingredients.

The greatest method for food to finish at once is using Smart Finish.
I detest it when my food cooks at various times. My issues have a remedy in Smart Finish. Consider that cooking the chicken in a single basket takes longer than cooking the vegetables. Regardless of the time or temperature, I simply push Smart Complete to have the air fryer finish frying both baskets at once. When it's finished, I'll have hot meals that I can serve without having to reheat it beforehand. This is how it goes:
When preparing items with various cook times, temperatures, or even functions, to finish cooking at the same time:

1. Fill the baskets with ingredients, then put the baskets inside the apparatus.
2. Zone 1 will continue to be lit up. Choose the cooking option that you want. Set the temperature using the TEMP arrows, and the time with the TIME arrows.
3. Then choose the desired cooking function after choosing zone 2. (If zone 1 is chosen, AIR BROIL is not an option.) Set the temperature using the TEMP arrows, and the time with the TIME arrows.
4. To start cooking in the zone with the most time, press SMART FINISH, then push the START/PAUSE button. Hold will be seen in the opposite zone. When both zones have the same amount of time left, the unit will beep and activate the second zone.
5. The appliance will beep and "End" will show up on the display when cooking is finished.
6. Utilize tongs or utensils with a silicone tip to remove the ingredients. Don't put a drawer on top of the appliance.

Match Cook provides more room.
Most likely, you've heard about how wonderful air-fried chicken wings are. Crispy on the outside and juicy on the inside, they are the ideal wing. The only issue is how much room wings can take up in your air fryer. The greatest method I discovered for spreading out my food in the baskets for even cooking without cramming was to use the Match Cook setting on my Ninja Foodie. This is how it goes:

1. Select your preferred method of cooking: air fry, roast, reheat, or dehydrate.
2. Choose the temperature and time.
3. Select MATCH COOK to get going. Numbers 1 and 2 will both turn on.
4. Click START/PAUSE to begin.
5. "End" will appear on both screens when cooking ends at the same time.
6. Remove ingredients by dumping them out or using silicone-tipped tongs or utensils.

When using Smart Finish and Match Cook, Ninja offers two stickers on the air fryer with suggested timings and temperatures for frying poultry and vegetables in case you ever wonder what settings to use. These recipes for air fryers are also useful.

A single zone for the cook time to end (while using both zones): Pick the area where you want to stop. To reset the time to zero, push the down arrow on the TIME button. Press the START/PAUSE button once you have reset the time to zero. After that, the time in that zone is cancelled, and the word "End" will show up on the display. The other area will still be used for cooking.

Pushing off both zones at once: Press the START/PAUSE button to pause time in the SMART FINISH mode or to pause both zones in dual zone cooking. Press the START/PAUSE button once again to resume cooking.

Pushing a single zone while cooking in a dual-zone: Select the zone you want to halt time in, then press the START/PAUSE button while both zones are still active.

Tips for using accessories

1. Each perforated parchment paper for the Ninja Foodi air fryer enables hot air to circulate around the meal. For Air Fryer. Additionally, the air fryer liner can effectively prevent the majority of food residue from making direct contact with the air fryer basket, making it easier for you to clean the air fryer.
2. Silicone Heat Resistant Pad for Ninja Foodi DZ201 air fryer are heat-resistant up to 230°C. These heat-resistant pads precisely grip the air fryer basket when you're through cooking and remove it, protecting the countertop from splitting from the heat.
3. When you think you've prepared the ideal food, record it using these DIY-edited air fryer cooking stickers so you can recreate it flawlessly the following time. Additionally, it makes it simpler for you to explain to your friends how you prepare food.
4. Please take note that if you use these air fryer paper liners by themselves during the preheating stage, the strong air could blow them away and cause them to come in contact with the hot elements. Additionally, add enough food to the parchment to keep it firmly attached to the bottom of the air fryer basket and prevent it from blowing away.

Cleaning and Caring

The crisper trays and their accompanying baskets were simple to wash by hand and dishwasher-safe. The trays fit easily in the dishwasher, but the large baskets and their handles got in the way. I once used the dishwasher to clean the baskets, but I actually preferred hand washing them.

Primary Unit: Wipe a moist towel over the main unit and the control panel to clean them. NEVER submerge the main unit in water or any other liquid, it should be noted.

Crisper Plates Crisper plates: Crisper Plates Crisper plates can be hand-washed or put in the dishwasher. After using, air-dry or towel-dry all portions if you washed them by hand.

Baskets: You have two options for washing baskets: by hand or in the dishwasher. After using, air-dry or towel-dry all portions if you washed them by hand. We advise hand-washing your baskets to increase their lifespan.

FAQ & Notes

How can I change the time or the temperature in a specific zone?
By pressing the up/down arrows while a single zone is operating, the time or temperature can be changed whenever you like.

How can I change the time or the temperature while using both zones?
Use the TEMP arrows to change the temperature or the TIME arrows to change the time after choosing the desired zone.

Can I prepare different dishes without worrying about cross-contamination in each zone?
Yes, each zones have independent heating elements and fans and are self-contained.

When using both zones, how can I pause or stop one?
Press the START/PAUSE button after choosing the zone you want to pause or stop.

Can I safely place the baskets on my countertop?
During cooking, the baskets will warm up. Handle them carefully, and only put them on surfaces that can withstand heat. The baskets SHOULD NOT be positioned on the unit's top.

I have a crisper plate. When should I use it?
Whenever you want your meal to be crisp, use the crisper plate. The plate raises the contents of the basket so that air can circulate beneath and around it, evenly cooking the food.

Why did my food not finish cooking?
During cooking, make sure the basket is fully inserted. Make sure the ingredients are layered evenly and without overlap on the bottom of the basket for uniform browning. Toss ingredients with a shake to ensure even crispness. You can alter the cooking temperature and duration at any moment. To change the temperature or the time, merely use the TEMP or TIME arrows.

How come my food gets burned?
For the best results, keep an eye on the food while it cooks and remove it when the ideal level of brownness is reached. To prevent overcooking, remove food from the unit as soon as the cook time is over.

When air frying, why do some components flutter about?
On occasion, the air fryer's fan will fling light meals in all directions. To hold loose, light food, such as the top piece of bread on a sandwich, in place, use wooden toothpicks.

Can I cook wet, battered ingredients in the air?
Yes, but make sure you bread your food properly. It's crucial to coat meals with flour, egg, and then bread crumbs in that order. To prevent crumbs from being blown off by the fan, press the breading firmly onto the battered items.

What caused the screen to go black?
The device is set to standby. Simply push the power button to restart it.

Why does the device beep?
The dish has either finished cooking or the other zone has begun.

Does a two-basket air fryer perform better?
One drawback of single-air fryers is that only one type of food may be cooked at a time in comparatively tiny batches. A dual-air fryer has a little more versatility because it can cook several dishes simultaneously at various temperatures.

In a Ninja Foodi 2-basket air fryer, is baking possible?
With the Ninja Foodi 2-Basket Air Fryer, what can I cook? This Ninja twin air fryer does six other tasks in addition to crisping up your french fries with less oil. Additionally, it can roast, bake, dehydrate, broil, and reheat.

Notes
1. Ensure that the ingredients are layered evenly and without overlap on the bottom of the basket for uniform browning. Midway during the cooking process, make sure to shake any overlapping ingredients.
2. You can alter the cooking temperature and duration at any moment. Simply select the zone you want to modify, then change the temperature or the time by using the TEMP or TIME arrows.
3. Lower the temperature by 25°F in order to adapt recipes from a conventional oven. To prevent overcooking, periodically check your food.
4. On sometimes, the air fryer's fan will fling light meals in all directions. Secure food with wooden toothpicks (such as the top piece of bread on a sandwich) to help with this.
5. The crisper plates raise the food in the baskets so that air can flow underneath and around it to provide even, crisp results.
6. You can push the START/PAUSE button to start cooking right away after choosing a cooking function. The temperature and time settings on the device will be used.
7. Use at least 1 tablespoon of oil when cooking fresh veggies and potatoes for the best results. To obtain the required level of crispiness, add extra oil as needed.
8. To get the best results, keep an eye on tthe food while it cooks and take it out when the ideal level of brownness has been reached. To keep track of the internal temperature of proteins, we advise using an instant-read thermometer.
9. To achieve the best results and prevent overcooking, remove food as soon as the cooking time is up.

4-Week Diet Plan

Week 1

Day 1:
Breakfast: Savory Scotch Eggs
Lunch: Creamy Pesto Potato
Snack: Spiced Mixed Nuts
Dinner: Lemony Turkey Breasts with Basil
Dessert: Coconut Squash Pie

Day 2:
Breakfast: Breakfast Sausage Patties
Lunch: Savory Samosas
Snack: Paprika Pumpkin Seeds
Dinner: Honey Soy Sauce Pork Chops
Dessert: Lemony Coconut Poppy Seed Macaroons

Day 3:
Breakfast: Cheddar Kale-Olive Mix
Lunch: Easy Potatoes
Snack: Spiced Shrimp with Bacon
Dinner: Sweet Paprika Cod with Endives
Dessert: Cream Plum Delight

Day 4:
Breakfast: Paprika Radish Hash Browns
Lunch: Buttered Pumpkin Seed Brown Bread
Snack: Tomato Bacon Smokies
Dinner: Yogurt Caramelized Eggplant
Dessert: Lemony Strawberries

Day 5:
Breakfast: Mustard Syrup Ham Steaks
Lunch: Garlic Asparagus
Snack: Paprika Butter Roasted Carrots
Dinner: Cheesy-Mayo Ham Chicken Breasts
Dessert: Butter Apple & Pecans Pie Bread Pudding

Day 6:
Breakfast: Spinach Prosciutto Egg Cups
Lunch: Cheesy Coconut Biscuits
Snack: Coconut Shrimp Balls
Dinner: Lime Sea Bass with Tomato and Okra
Dessert: Tasty Cinnamon Bananas

Day 7:
Breakfast: Cheesy Tomato Frittata
Lunch: Herbed Butter Radishes
Snack: Dill Eggplant Chips
Dinner: Homemade Pork Chops
Dessert: Buttered Raisin Bread Pudding

Week 2

Day 1:
Breakfast: Spinach & Bacon Spread
Lunch: Cheesy Green Bean Casserole
Snack: Crispy Cheese Zucchini Chips
Dinner: Homemade Chicken Parmesan
Dessert: Sweet Raspberry Doughnuts

Day 2:
Breakfast: Crispy Bacon
Lunch: Cheesy Zucchini ChipsCheesy Zucchini Chips
Snack: Spicy Avocado Balls
Dinner: Garlic Pork Loin with Potatoes
Dessert: Vanilla Coconut Cream Pie

Day 3:
Breakfast: Eggplant-Spinach Frittata
Lunch: Cheesy Beet & Spinach Salad
Snack: Cheesy Green Bean Fries
Dinner: Coconut Catfish Bites
Dessert: Whipped Cream Vanilla Cake

Day 4:
Breakfast: Simple Sweet Potato Veggie Hash
Lunch: Lemony Charred Shishito Peppers
Snack: Hot-Spicy Chicken Drumettes
Dinner: Bacon Wrapped Halibut
Dessert: Lemony Cheese Mini Pies

Day 5:
Breakfast: Sweet Buttered Doughnuts
Lunch: Spicy-Sweet Brussels Sprouts
Snack: Dijon & Quinoa Tomato Meatballs
Dinner: Chili Garlic Pork Spareribs
Dessert: Chocolate Coconut Bread Pudding

Day 6:
Breakfast: Cheesy Green Chili & Egg Bites
Lunch: Garlic Vegetable Spring Rolls
Snack: Crunchy Almond Coconut Granola
Dinner: Coconut Turmeric Chicken Strips
Dessert: Cinnamon Apple & Cranberry Dumplings

Day 7:
Breakfast: Cheesy Veggie Omelet
Lunch: Homemade Flatbread
Snack: Cocktail Flanks Rolls
Dinner: Delicious Pork Loin with Sweet Potatoes
Dessert: Cheesy Orange Almond Fritters

Week 3

Day 1:
Breakfast: Cheesy Spinach Muffins
Lunch: Classic Dinner Rolls
Snack: Cheesy Broccoli & Egg Balls
Dinner: Garlicky Buttery Haddock
Dessert: Lemony Banana Beignets

Day 2:
Breakfast: Cheesy Buttered Corn Bread
Lunch: Lime Chili Cauliflower
Snack: Cheesy Chicken Zucchini Boats
Dinner: Classic Nashville Hot Chicken
Dessert: Coconut Strawberry Cake with Almond

Day 3:
Breakfast: Healthy Eggs Ramekins
Lunch: Delicious Cheesy Cauliflower Tots
Snack: Cheesy Butter Brussels Sprouts
Dinner: Mustard Tuna Steak
Dessert: Mini Orange Raspberry Tarts

Day 4:
Breakfast: Eggs in Peppers Cups
Lunch: Easy Roasted Garlic
Snack: Crispy Cheesy Cauliflower
Dinner: Crispy Pork Chops
Dessert: Lemony Curd Pavlova with Blueberries

Day 5:
Breakfast: Cheesy Crustless Mini Quiches
Lunch: Tasty Semolina Veggie Cutlets
Snack: Simple Sprouts Wraps
Dinner: Spicy Cod Fillets
Dessert: Yummy Chocolate Avocado

Day 6:
Breakfast: Mozzarella Pepperoni Rolls
Lunch: Cheesy Sausage-Stuffed Mushroom Caps
Snack: French Vermouth Mushrooms
Dinner: Hoisin Butted Turkey Drumstick
Dessert: Sweet Cinnamon Chickpeas

Day 7:
Breakfast: Cheesy Spinach-Stuffed French Toast
Lunch: Honey Charred Sweet Potatoes
Snack: Pickled Dill Bacon Bowls
Dinner: Lemony Pork Belly Roast
Dessert: Cinnamon Peach Cake

Week 4

Day 1:
Breakfast: Lime Avocado Salad
Lunch: Cheesy Asparagus & Mushroom Soufflés
Snack: Ricotta Balls with Chives
Dinner: Creamy Haddock Fillet
Dessert: Coconut Nuts Cookies

Day 2:
Breakfast: Cheesy Puffy Egg Tarts
Lunch: Spicy Tahini Kale Leaves
Snack: Easy Pork Rinds
Dinner: Super-Easy Chicken Breasts
Dessert: Vanilla Plum Dessert

Day 3:
Breakfast: Easy Cheesy Frittata
Lunch: Mole-Braised Chili Cauliflower
Snack: Sweet-Spicy Spare Ribs
Dinner: Onion Pumpkin & Pork Empanadas
Dessert: Butter Chocolate Mini Cheesecakes

Day 4:
Breakfast: Garlic Sweet Potatoes
Lunch: Crispy Onion Pakora
Snack: Lemony Sage Potatoes
Dinner: Coconut Cream Salmon
Dessert: Creamy Peach & Almond Dessert

Day 5:
Breakfast: Simple Eggs
Lunch: Buttered Potato, Cauliflower and Pea Turnovers
Snack: Delicious Roasted Parsnip
Dinner: Lemony Chili Octopus
Dessert: Healthy Fresh Fruit Crumble

Day 6:
Breakfast: Cinnamon French Toast Sticks
Lunch: Homemade Potato Tots
Snack: Juicy Chocolate Bacon Bites
Dinner: Spicy Chicken-Lettuce Sandwich
Dessert: Vanilla Cocoa Bombs

Day 7:
Breakfast: Cheesy Ham Breakfast Pockets
Lunch: Caesar Cheesy Whole Cauliflower
Snack: Cheesy Mushrooms with Chives
Dinner: Basil Cheese Pork Balls
Dessert: Chocolate Cream-Filled Mini Cakes

Chapter 1 Breakfast

Cheesy Crustless Mini Quiches

Prep Time: 20 minutes | Cook Time: 15 minutes | Serves: 3

6 large eggs
¼ cup sour cream
1 tablespoon cornstarch
½ cup frozen shredded hash brown potatoes, thawed

½ cup shredded Swiss cheese
½ cup shredded Colby cheese
1 scallion, chopped
1 tablespoon minced fresh chives

1. Install the crisper plate in both baskets, place the 6 silicone muffin cups in the baskets, and insert the baskets into the unit. Set aside. 2. Beat the eggs until scrambled in a large bowl. Add the sour cream and cornstarch to stir well. 3. Add the potatoes, scallion, Swiss cheese, Colby cheese, and chives and mix well. 4. Using a ¼-cup measure, divide the mixture among the muffin cups in the basket. 5. Select Zone 1 and select BAKE. Then set the temperature to 325°F and set the time to 15 minutes. Then select MATCH COOK to match the Settings in Zone 2 with those in Zone 1. Select START/PAUSE to begin. Bake for 15 minutes or until the quiches are puffed and light golden brown. 6. Once cooking has finished, Serve.

Per Serving: Calories 380; Fat 24.96g; Sodium 315mg; Carbs 12.88g; Fiber 0.7g; Sugar 0.95g; Protein 25.23g

Eggs in Peppers Cups

Prep Time: 10 minutes | Cook Time: 12 minutes | Serves: 12

6 green bell peppers
12 eggs

½ teaspoon ground black pepper
½ teaspoon chili flakes

1. Cut the green bell peppers into halves and remove the seeds. 2. Then crack the eggs in every bell pepper half and sprinkle with ground black pepper and chili flakes. 3. Install the crisper plate in both baskets, place the green bell pepper halves in the baskets, and insert the baskets into the unit. 4. Select Zone 1 and select AIR FRY. Then set the temperature to 395°F and set the time to 4 minutes. Select MATCH COOK to match the Settings in Zone 2 with those in Zone 1. Then select START/PAUSE to begin. 5. Once cooking has finished, serve.

Per Serving: Calories 73; Fat 4.25g; Sodium 68mg; Carbs 2.68g; Fiber 0.4g; Sugar 1.41g; Protein 6.03g

Breakfast Sausage Patties

Prep Time: 15 minutes | Cook Time: 20 minutes | Serves: 4

1 pound ground pork
1 teaspoon salt
1 teaspoon freshly ground black pepper
¾ teaspoon garlic powder

½ teaspoon ground sage
¼ teaspoon ground thyme
¼ teaspoon ground red pepper flakes

1. Add the pork, thyme, black pepper, garlic powder, salt, sage, and red pepper flakes in a large bowl. Mix the seasonings evenly into the pork with the hands. Avoid overworking the meat. 2. Divide the seasoned pork into ¼-cup portions, roll every portion into a ball, and press it down slightly to form a patty. 3. Install the crisper plate in both baskets, place the patties in a single layer in the baskets, leaving a little space between each to ensure even cooking, and insert the baskets into the unit. 4. Select Zone 1 and select AIR FRY. Then set the temperature to 400°F and set the time to 10 minutes. Select MATCH COOK to match the Settings in Zone 2 with those in Zone 1. Select START/PAUSE to begin. 5. Cook for 10 minutes. Pause to flip the patties and cook for another 5 to 8 minutes until the pork reaches an internal temperature of 160°F. 6. Once cooking has finished, serve.

Per Serving: Calories 303; Fat 24.08g; Sodium 646mg; Carbs 1.22g; Fiber 0.3g; Sugar 0.16g; Protein 19.38g

Cheesy Spinach–Stuffed French Toast

Prep Time: 15 minutes | Cook Time: 8 minutes | Serves: 4

½ cup shredded Havarti cheese
½ cup frozen spinach, thawed and well-drained
4 tablespoons (2 ounces) cream cheese, at room temperature
2 scallions, chopped
1 garlic clove, minced
½ teaspoon dried marjoram

¼ teaspoon sea salt
⅛ teaspoon freshly ground black pepper
4 (1¼-inch-thick) slices French bread
2 large eggs
¼ cup whole milk
½ cup dried bread crumbs

1. In a medium bowl, combine the Havarti, cream cheese, spinach, scallions, garlic, salt, marjoram, and pepper and mix well. 2. Cut a slit in the side of each piece of French bread about 2 inches wide. 3. Stuff the pockets with the spinach mixture. Press the slices gently to close. 4. Beat the eggs with the milk until smooth in a shallow bowl. Place the French bread slices into the egg mixture, turning once, letting the bread absorb most of the egg mixture. 5. Place the bread crumbs on a plate. Dip the egg-soaked bread slices into the bread crumbs; pat down on them so they adhere to the slices. 6. Install the crisper plate in the basket, place the bread slices in the basket, and insert the basket into the unit. Select Zone 1 and select BAKE. Then set the temperature to 350°F and set the time to 8 minutes. Select START/PAUSE to begin. Cook for 3 to 4 minutes on each side, turning once, until the bread is browned and crisp. 7. Once cooking has finished, serve.
Per Serving: Calories 260; Fat 12. 82g; Sodium 560mg; Carbs 25. 11g; Fiber 1. 8g; Sugar 4. 22g; Protein 11. 77g

Cheesy Spinach Muffins

Prep Time: 5 minutes | Cook Time: 15 minutes | Serves: 4

2 eggs, whisked
Cooking spray
1 and ½ cups coconut milk
1 tablespoon baking powder

4 ounces baby spinach, chopped
2 ounces parmesan cheese, grated
3 ounces almond flour

1. Mix all the ingredients except the cooking spray in a bowl and whisk really well. 2. Grease the muffin pans that fit the air fryer with the cooking spray and divide the muffins mix. 3. Install the crisper plate in both baskets, place the muffin pans in the baskets, and insert the baskets into the unit. 4. Select Zone 1 and select AIR FRY. Then set the temperature to 380°F and set the time to 15 minutes. Select MATCH COOK to match the Settings in Zone 2 with those in Zone 1. Then select START/PAUSE to begin. 5. Once cooking has finished, divide between plates and serve.
Per Serving: Calories 369; Fat 31. 84g; Sodium 322mg; Carbs 12. 83g; Fiber 4. 7g; Sugar 3. 14g; Protein 13. 48g

Mozzarella Pepperoni Rolls

Prep Time: 15 minutes | Cook Time: 6 minutes | Serves: 6

6 wonton wrappers
1 tablespoon keto tomato sauce
½ cup Mozzarella, shredded

1 oz pepperoni, chopped
1 egg, beaten
Cooking spray

1. In the big bowl, mix the pepperoni, shredded Mozzarella, and tomato sauce. 2. When the mixture is homogenous, transfer it on the wonton wraps. 3. Wrap the wonton wraps in the shape of sticks. Then brush them with beaten eggs. 4. Spray the crisper plate with cooking spray. Install the crisper plate in the basket, place the pizza sticks in the basket, and insert the basket into the unit. 5. Select Zone 1 and select AIR FRY. Then set the temperature to 400°F and set the time to 3 minutes. Select START/PAUSE to begin. Cook them for 3 minutes from each side. 6. Once cooking has finished, serve.
Per Serving: Calories 160; Fat 4. 61g; Sodium 394mg; Carbs 19. 57g; Fiber 0. 9g; Sugar 0. 44g; Protein 9. 08g

Cheesy Green Chili & Egg Bites

Prep Time: 10 minutes | Cook Time: 10 minutes | Serves: 4

Extra-virgin olive oil, for the molds
5 large eggs
2 tablespoons milk
½ cup shredded pepper Jack cheese

1 (4-ounce) can diced green chilies, drained
¼ teaspoon salt
⅛ teaspoon freshly ground black pepper

1. Lightly spray a silicone egg bites mold with oil. Install the egg bites in the both baskets. 2. Whisk together the milk and eggs in a medium bowl. Stir in the green chilies, salt, cheese, and pepper. 3. Pour 1 tablespoon of the egg mixture into each section of the egg mold until they are about half full. Carefully place the egg mold in the baskets and insert the baskets into the unit. 4. Select Zone 1 and select AIR FRY. Then set the temperature to 350°F and set the time to 10 minutes. Select MATCH COOK to match the Settings in Zone 2 with those in Zone 1. Select START/PAUSE to begin. Cook for 8 to 10 minutes until the tops are lightly browned and the egg is set. 5. Once cooking has finished, serve.
Per Serving: Calories 181; Fat 13. 01g; Sodium 428mg; Carbs 2. 16g; Fiber 0. 7g; Sugar 0. 73g; Protein 13. 54g

Cheesy Puffy Egg Tarts

Prep Time: 5 minutes | Cook Time: 40 minutes | Serves: 4

2 tablespoons all-purpose flour
1 sheet frozen puff pastry, thawed
Extra-virgin olive oil, for the basket
1 cup shredded Monterey Jack cheese

4 large eggs
Salt
Freshly ground black pepper
1 tablespoon minced chives (optional)

1. Lightly flour the work surface. Unfold the thawed puff pastry sheet and cut it into 4 equal squares. 2. Lightly spray the crisper plate with oil. Place 4 puff pastry squares in the baskets. Install the baskets into the unit. 3. Select Zone 1 and select AIR FRY. Then set the temperature to 380°F and set the time to 10 minutes. Select MATCH COOK to match the Settings in Zone 2 with those in Zone 1. Select START/PAUSE to begin. Cook for 8 to 10 minutes until golden brown. 4. Open the air fryer. Use a spoon to press down the center of the squares so there is a nice indentation. Sprinkle ¼ cup shredded cheese into the indentation in each square. Carefully crack an egg on top of the cheese. Season with salt and pepper. 5. Cook for another 10 minutes until the eggs are cooked to your preference. 6. Top the egg tarts with chives, if using. 7. Once cooking has finished, serve.
Per Serving: Calories 265; Fat 19. 79g; Sodium 817mg; Carbs 9. 51g; Fiber 0. 4g; Sugar 0. 38g; Protein 12. 12g

Simple Eggs

Prep Time: 8 minutes | Cook Time: 16 minutes | Serves: 2

4 eggs

¼ teaspoon salt

1. Install the crisper plate in the basket, place the eggs in the basket, and insert the basket into the unit. 2. Select Zone 1 and select AIR FRY. Then set the temperature to 250°F and set the time to 16 minutes. Select START/PAUSE to begin. 3. When the eggs are cooked, cool them in the ice water. After this, peel the eggs and cut into halves. Sprinkle the eggs with salt.
Per Serving: Calories 126; Fat 8. 37g; Sodium 416mg; Carbs 0. 63g; Fiber 0g; Sugar 0. 33g; Protein 11. 05g

Easy Cheesy Frittata

Prep Time: 10 minutes | Cook Time: 20 minutes | Serves: 6

1 cup almond milk
Cooking spray
9 ounces cream cheese, soft
1 cup cheddar cheese, shredded

6 spring onions, chopped
Salt and black pepper to the taste
6 eggs, whisked

1. Grease the crisper plate with the cooking spray. 2. Mix the eggs with the rest of the ingredients in a bowl and whisk well. 3. Install the crisper plate in the basket, spread the mixture to the basket, and insert the basket into the unit. 4. Select Zone 1 and select AIR FRY. Then set the temperature to 350°F and set the time to 20 minutes. Select START/PAUSE to begin. 5. Once cooking has finished, divide everything between plates and serve.
Per Serving: Calories 366; Fat 30. 04g; Sodium 318mg; Carbs 6. 04g; Fiber 0. 5g; Sugar 4. 6g; Protein 18. 11g

Spinach & Bacon Spread

Prep Time: 5 minutes | Cook Time: 10 minutes | Serves: 4

2 tablespoons coconut cream
3 cups spinach leaves
2 tablespoons cilantro

2 tablespoons bacon, cooked and crumbled
Salt and black pepper to the taste

1. Install the crisper plate in the basket, place all the ingredients in the basket, except the bacon. 2. Insert the basket into the unit. Select Zone 1 and select AIR FRY. Then set the temperature to 360°F and set the time to 10 minutes. Select START/PAUSE to begin. 3. Once cooking has finished, transfer to a blender, pulse well, divide into bowls and serve with bacon sprinkled on top.
Per Serving: Calories 45; Fat 4. 04g; Sodium 666mg; Carbs 1. 99g; Fiber 0. 9g; Sugar 0. 1g; Protein 1. 47g

Cheesy Buttered Corn Bread

Prep Time: 15 minutes | Cook Time: 22 minutes | Serves: 4

Nonstick baking spray containing flour
⅔ cup yellow cornmeal
½ cup all-purpose flour
1 teaspoon baking powder
½ teaspoon baking soda
¼ teaspoon sea salt

½ cup shredded Cheddar cheese
1 cup buttermilk
2 large eggs
¼ cup butter, melted
1 tablespoon honey

1. Spray the crisper plates with the baking spray and set aside. 2. Combine the cornmeal, baking powder, flour, baking soda, and salt in a medium bowl. Add the cheese and toss to coat. 3. In a glass measuring cup, combine the eggs, buttermilk, butter, and honey until smooth. Place this mixture into the flour mixture and stir until combined. 4. Install the crisper plate in both baskets. Spread the batter into the prepared plates. Insert the baskets into the unit. Select Zone 1 and select BAKE. Then set the temperature to 350°F and set the time to 22 minutes. Select START/PAUSE to begin. 5. Bake for 17 to 22 minutes until the bread is golden brown and a toothpick inserted in the center comes out clean. 6. Once cooking has finished, let cool for 15 minutes before cutting into four wedges to serve.
Per Serving: Calories 407; Fat 21. 38g; Sodium 656mg; Carbs 41. 07g; Fiber 1. 5g; Sugar 7. 86g; Protein 12. 76g

Savory Scotch Eggs

Prep Time: 20 minutes | Cook Time: 10 minutes | Serves: 4

1 pound bulk pork sausage
1 tablespoon finely chopped chives
1 teaspoon dried minced onion
½ teaspoon salt
½ teaspoon freshly ground black pepper

¼ cup all-purpose flour
1 large egg
¾ cup panko bread crumbs
4 hard-boiled eggs
Extra-virgin olive oil, for spraying

1. In a medium bowl, add the sausage, onion, salt, chives, and pepper. Gently mix until well combined. 2. Shape the mixture into 4 equal-size patties. 3. Put the flour into a small shallow bowl. 4. In a second small shallow bowl, beat the egg. 5. Put the bread crumbs in a third small shallow bowl. 6. Pat dry the hard-boiled eggs with a paper towel. Roll each egg in the flour to coat. 7. Place one flour-coated egg on each sausage patty. Wrap the sausage patty around the egg so it completely encases the egg. 8. Coat the sausage-encased egg in the beaten egg, then in the bread crumbs. 9. Lightly spray the crisper plate with oil. Install the crisper plate in both baskets, place the Scotch eggs in a single layer in the baskets, lightly spray with oil and insert the baskets into the unit. 10. Select Zone 1 and select AIR FRY. Then set the temperature to 400°F and set the time to 6 minutes. Select MATCH COOK to match the Settings in Zone 2 with those in Zone 1. Select START/PAUSE to begin. 11. Cook for 6 minutes. Flip the Scotch eggs and lightly spray with oil. Cook for another 5 to 6 minutes until the sausage is fully cooked. 12. Once cooking has finished, serve.
Per Serving: Calories 620; Fat 47. 49g; Sodium 1279mg; Carbs 17. 58g; Fiber 1. 2g; Sugar 5. 26g; Protein 28. 81g

Crispy Bacon

Prep Time: 15 minutes | Cook Time: 10 minutes | Serves: 4

8 slices bacon

1. Install the crisper plate in both baskets, place the bacon in the baskets, and insert the baskets into the unit. 2. Select Zone 1 and select AIR FRY. Then set the temperature to 350°F and set the time to 10 minutes. Select MATCH COOK to match the Settings in Zone 2 with those in Zone 1. Select START/PAUSE to begin. 3. Cook for 5 minutes. Check the bacon for doneness and rearrange if it is no longer in a single layer. Cook for another 3 to 5 minutes until crispy and lightly browned. 4. Once cooking has finished, serve.
Per Serving: Calories 212; Fat 20. 42g; Sodium 244mg; Carbs 0. 43g; Fiber 0g; Sugar 0. 43g; Protein 6. 52g

Simple Sweet Potato Veggie Hash

Prep Time: 15 minutes | Cook Time: 28 minutes | Serves: 4

1 tablespoon olive oil
3 Yukon Gold potatoes, peeled and chopped
1 sweet potato, peeled and chopped
1 yellow onion, diced
1 red bell pepper, diced

2 garlic cloves, sliced
1 teaspoon dried thyme
½ teaspoon sea salt
⅛ teaspoon freshly ground black pepper

1. In a medium bowl, toss the olive oil with the Yukon Gold and sweet potatoes. Install the crisper plate in the basket, place the mixture in the basket, and insert the basket into the unit. 2. Select Zone 1 and select BAKE. Then set the temperature to 400°F and set the time to 15 minutes. Select START/PAUSE to begin. Cook until they are tender. 3. Add the onion, garlic, bell pepper, thyme, salt, and pepper to the basket to toss. 4. Bake for 8 to 13 minutes longer and stir halfway through cooking time, until the potatoes are browned and crisp and the vegetables are crisp-tender. 5. Once cooking has finished, serve.
Per Serving: Calories 265; Fat 3. 76g; Sodium 310mg; Carbs 53. 29g; Fiber 7. 3g; Sugar 3. 94g; Protein 6. 44g

Garlic Sweet Potatoes

Prep Time: 15 minutes | Cook Time: 30 minutes | Serves: 4

2 medium russet potatoes, peeled and cut into ½-inch chunks
2 medium sweet potatoes, peeled and cut into ½-inch chunks

1 tablespoon extra-virgin olive oil, plus more for spraying
2 teaspoons minced garlic
2 teaspoons seasoned salt
½ teaspoon freshly ground black pepper

1. In a large bowl, add the russet potatoes and sweet potatoes. Toss with the olive oil, seasoned salt, garlic, and pepper. 2. Lightly spray the crisper plate with oil. Install the crisper plate in the basket, place the seasoned potatoes in the basket, and insert the basket into the unit. 3. Select Zone 1 and select AIR FRY. Then set the temperature to 400°F and set the time to 30 minutes. Select START/PAUSE to begin. Cook for 25 to 30 minutes. Shake the air fryer basket every 5 to 10 minutes and lightly spray the potatoes with oil. Cook until nicely browned and slightly crisp. 4. Once cooking has finished, serve.
Per Serving: Calories 236; Fat 3. 67g; Sodium 1193mg; Carbs 47. 42g; Fiber 4. 4g; Sugar 5. 49g; Protein 5. 11g

Mustard Syrup Ham Steaks

Prep Time: 5 minutes | Cook Time: 15 minutes | Serves: 4

2 tablespoons maple syrup
½ tablespoon apple cider vinegar
½ tablespoon Dijon mustard

¼ tablespoon brown sugar
1 (1-pound) ham steak, fully cooked

1. In a small bowl, whisk together the vinegar, maple syrup, mustard, and brown sugar. 2. Install the crisper plate in the basket. Remove the ham from the package and place in the basket, and insert the basket into the unit. Brush the marinade evenly over the top of the ham. 3. Select Zone 1 and select AIR FRY. Then set the temperature to 380°F and set the time to 6 minutes. Select START/PAUSE to begin. Cook for 6 minutes. Flip the ham and brush with more marinade. Cook for another 6 to 8 minutes, or until the ham is lightly browned and the glaze is caramelized. 4. Once cooking has finished, serve.
Per Serving: Calories 145; Fat 3. 93g; Sodium 1473mg; Carbs 8. 43g; Fiber 0. 1g; Sugar 6. 54g; Protein 19. 24g

Lime Avocado Salad

Prep Time: 10 minutes | Cook Time: 3 minutes | Serves: 4

1 avocado, peeled, pitted and roughly sliced
½ teaspoon minced garlic
¼ teaspoon chili flakes
½ teaspoon olive oil
1 tablespoon lime juice

¼ teaspoon salt
1 teaspoon cilantro, chopped
1 cup baby spinach
1 cup cherry tomatoes halved
Cooking spray

1. Install the crisper plate in the basket and spray the inside of plate with cooking spray. 2. Combine all the ingredients in the basket, and insert the basket into the unit. Select Zone 1 and select AIR FRY. Then set the temperature to 400°F and set the time to 3 minutes. Select START/PAUSE to begin. 3. Once cooking has finished, divide into bowls and serve.
Per Serving: Calories 118; Fat 8. 81g; Sodium 164mg; Carbs 10. 54g; Fiber 4. 3g; Sugar 5. 08g; Protein 1. 75g

Sweet Buttered Doughnuts
Prep Time: 10 minutes | Cook Time: 10 minutes | Serves: 4

1 tablespoon ground cinnamon
⅔ cup granulated sugar
1 (8-count) can large flaky biscuits

Extra-virgin olive oil, for the basket
5 tablespoons butter, melted

1. In a small bowl, add the cinnamon and sugar. Set aside. 2. Take out the biscuits from the can and place on a sheet of parchment paper. Use a 1-inch round biscuit cutter or a bottle cap to cut a hole out of the center of each biscuit to make a doughnut. 3. Lightly spray the crisper plate with oil and install the crisper plate in both baskets. Place the doughnuts in a single layer in the basket, leaving ½ inch between each to ensure even cooking, not discard the parchment paper. Insert the baskets into the unit. 4. Select Zone 1 and select AIR FRY. Then set the temperature to 350°F and set the time to 7 minutes. Select MATCH COOK to match the Settings in Zone 2 with those in Zone 1. Select START/PAUSE to begin. 5. Cook for 5 to 7 minutes until golden brown. 6. Once cooking has finished, transfer the doughnuts back to the parchment paper. Brush with the melted butter, making sure to coat all sides. 7. Dip each doughnut in the cinnamon-sugar mixture until well coated. 8. Serve the doughnuts warm. Put the leftovers in a covered container and store at room temperature for up to 3 days. Place the leftovers in the microwave and warm for 20 to 30 seconds.
Per Serving: Calories 269; Fat 17. 29g; Sodium 296mg; Carbs 28. 66g; Fiber 1. 3g; Sugar 17. 11g; Protein 1. 42g

Cheddar Kale–Olive Mix
Prep Time: 5 minutes | Cook Time: 20 minutes | Serves: 4

½ cup black olives, pitted and sliced
1 cup kale, chopped
2 tablespoons cheddar, grated

4 eggs, whisked
Cooking spray
A pinch of salt and black pepper

1. Mix the eggs with the rest of the ingredients in a bowl except the cooking spray and whisk well. 2. Grease the crisper plate with the cooking spray. Install the crisper plate in the basket, place the olives mixture in the basket and spread. 3. Insert the basket into the unit. Select Zone 1 and select AIR FRY. Then set the temperature to 360°F and set the time to 20 minutes. Select START/PAUSE to begin. 4. Once cooking has finished, serve for breakfast hot.
Per Serving: Calories 117; Fat 8. 83g; Sodium 812mg; Carbs 2. 14g; Fiber 0. 8g; Sugar 0. 28g; Protein 7. 49g

Cinnamon French Toast Sticks
Prep Time: 15 minutes | Cook Time: 10 minutes | Serves: 4

4 slices firm bread
2 large eggs
¼ cup milk
1 tablespoon brown sugar

1 teaspoon ground cinnamon
¼ teaspoon salt
2 teaspoons vanilla extract
Extra-virgin olive oil, for the basket

1. Cut each bread slice into 3 thick sticks, then set aside. 2. Whisk together the eggs, cinnamon, brown sugar, salt, milk, and vanilla in a medium shallow bowl until they form a smooth batter. 3. Dip each bread stick into the egg batter, making sure to coat all sides. 4. Lightly spray the crisper plate with oil. Install the crisper plate in both baskets, place the coated bread sticks in a single layer in the baskets, leaving ½ inch between each to ensure even cooking, and insert the baskets into the unit. 5. Select Zone 1 and select AIR FRY. Then set the temperature to 400°F and set the time to 4 minutes. Select MATCH COOK to match the Settings in Zone 2 with those in Zone 1. Select START/PAUSE to begin. 6. Cook for 4 minutes. Turn the sticks to cook for another 2 to 4 minutes until crispy and golden brown. 7. Once cooking has finished, serve.
Per Serving: Calories 112; Fat 4. 18g; Sodium 254mg; Carbs 13. 7g; Fiber 0. 9g; Sugar 4. 19g; Protein 3. 63g

Eggplant–Spinach Frittata

Prep Time: 5 minutes | Cook Time: 20 minutes | Serves: 4

1 tablespoon chives, chopped
1 eggplant, cubed
8 ounces spinach, torn

Cooking spray
6 eggs, whisked
Salt and black pepper to the taste

1. Mix the eggs with the rest of the ingredients except the cooking spray in a bowl and whisk well. 2. Grease the crisper plate with the cooking spray. Install the crisper plate in the basket, spread the frittata mix in the basket, and insert the basket into the unit. 3. Select Zone 1 and select AIR FRY. Then set the temperature to 380°F and set the time to 20 minutes. Select START/PAUSE to begin. 4. Once cooking has finished, divide between plates and serve for breakfast.

Per Serving: Calories 244; Fat 15. 66g; Sodium 782mg; Carbs 10. 71g; Fiber 4. 8g; Sugar 5. 27g; Protein 16. 28g

Spinach Prosciutto Egg Cups

Prep Time: 10 minutes | Cook Time: 15 minutes | Serves: 6

12 slices prosciutto
1½ cups fresh baby spinach leaves

12 medium eggs
Freshly ground black pepper

1. Press 1 slice of prosciutto into a silicone muffin cup so it creates a lining on the bottom and sides of the cup. Repeat with the remaining prosciutto. 2. Place 4 to 6 spinach leaves in the bottom of each cup. 3. Crack 1 egg into each cup and season with pepper. 4. Install the crisper plate in both baskets, place the muffin cups in the baskets, and insert the baskets into the unit. Cook in batches, depending on how many muffin cups your basket will hold. Do not overcrowd. 5. Select Zone 1 and select AIR FRY. Then set the temperature to 350°F and set the time to 15 minutes. Select MATCH COOK to match the Settings in Zone 2 with those in Zone 1. Select START/PAUSE to begin. 6. Cook for 10 to 15 minutes until the eggs are cooked to your preference. 7. Once cooking has finished, serve.

Per Serving: Calories 181; Fat 11. 52g; Sodium 330mg; Carbs 2. 39g; Fiber 0. 3g; Sugar 0. 98g; Protein 16. 29g

Cheesy Ham Quiche Cups

Prep Time: 10 minutes | Cook Time: 15 minutes | Serves: 6

Extra-virgin olive oil, for the muffin cups
6 large eggs, beaten
2 tablespoons milk
1 teaspoon minced garlic

½ teaspoon freshly ground black pepper
2 cups diced cooked ham
1 cup shredded Swiss cheese

1. Lightly spray 12 silicone muffin cups with olive oil. 2. In a medium bowl, whisk together the eggs and milk. Stir in the ham, garlic, pepper, and cheese. 3. Fill each muffin cup with ¼ cup of the mixture until they are approximately three-quarters full. 4. Install the crisper plate in both baskets, place the filled muffin cups in the baskets, leaving a little room between each to ensure even cooking, and insert the baskets into the unit. 5. Select Zone 1 and select AIR FRY. Then set the temperature to 330°F and set the time to 12 minutes. Select MATCH COOK to match the Settings in Zone 2 with those in Zone 1. Select START/PAUSE to begin. 6. Cook for 10 to 12 minutes until the eggs are set and tops are golden brown. 7. Once cooking has finished, serve.

Per Serving: Calories 209; Fat 13. 51g; Sodium 600mg; Carbs 2. 8g; Fiber 0. 1g; Sugar 1. 11g; Protein 18. 5g

Healthy Eggs Ramekins

Prep Time: 5 minutes | Cook Time: 6 minutes | Serves: 5

5 eggs
1 teaspoon coconut oil, melted

¼ teaspoon ground black pepper

1. Brush the ramekins with coconut oil and crack the eggs inside. Then sprinkle the eggs with ground black pepper. 2. Install the crisper plate in both baskets, place the ramekins in the baskets, and insert the baskets into the unit. 3. Select Zone 1 and select AIR FRY. Then set the temperature to 355°F and set the time to 6 minutes. Select MATCH COOK to match the Settings in Zone 2 with those in Zone 1. Then select START/PAUSE to begin. 4. Once cooking has finished, serve.

Per Serving: Calories 72; Fat 5. 1g; Sodium 63mg; Carbs 0. 53g; Fiber 0. 1g; Sugar 0. 16g; Protein 5. 56g

Paprika Radish Hash Browns

Prep Time: 20 minutes | Cook Time: 20 minutes | Serves: 4

2 pounds radishes
2 tablespoons extra-virgin olive oil, plus more for the basket
1½ teaspoons garlic powder

1½ teaspoons onion powder
1½ teaspoons paprika
1 teaspoon salt
1 teaspoon freshly ground black pepper

1. Cut the roots and stems off the radishes. 2. Cut the radishes into thin slices with a mandoline or food processor. 3. Place the radish slices with the olive oil, onion powder, paprika, salt, garlic powder, and pepper in a large bowl. Stir to evenly coat the radishes in the oil and seasonings. 4. Lightly spray the crisper plate with oil. Install the crisper plate in both baskets, place the half the seasoned radish slices in the baskets, and insert the baskets into the unit. 5. Select Zone 1 and select AIR FRY. Then set the temperature to 400°F and set the time to 5 minutes. Select MATCH COOK to match the Settings in Zone 2 with those in Zone 1. Select START/PAUSE to begin. 6. Cook for 5 minutes. Shake the basket to redistribute the hash browns. Lightly spray with oil and cook for another 5 minutes. 7. Once cooking has finished, serve.

Per Serving: Calories 112; Fat 7. 18g; Sodium 631mg; Carbs 11. 8g; Fiber 4. 4g; Sugar 5. 85g; Protein 1. 85g

Cheesy Egg Breakfast Bell Peppers

Prep Time: 15 minutes | Cook Time: 15 minutes | Serves: 4

2 red bell peppers
Salt
Freshly ground black pepper
4 tablespoons crumbled cooked bacon
8 tablespoons shredded mozzarella cheese

4 large eggs
Extra-virgin olive oil, for the basket
4 teaspoons finely chopped fresh chives, for garnish (optional)

1. Cut the bell peppers in half lengthwise from stem to base. 2. Pop out the stem, then remove the seeds and membranes so each half looks like a shallow bowl. 3. Season the inside of each bell pepper half with salt and black pepper. 4. Sprinkle 1 tablespoon chopped bacon into each bell pepper half, followed by 2 tablespoons mozzarella cheese. 5. Carefully crack one egg into each bell pepper half. 6. Lightly spray the crisper plate with oil. Install the crisper plate in both baskets, place the bell pepper halves in a single layer in the baskets, and insert the baskets into the unit. 7. Select Zone 1 and select AIR FRY. Then set the temperature to 350°F and set the time to 15 minutes. Select MATCH COOK to match the Settings in Zone 2 with those in Zone 1. Select START/PAUSE to begin. 8. Cook for 10 to 15 minutes until the eggs are cooked to your preference. 9. Once cooking has finished, sprinkle each stuffed pepper with 1 teaspoon chives, if using, and serve.

Per Serving: Calories 188; Fat 14. 52g; Sodium 1219mg; Carbs 6. 24g; Fiber 0. 7g; Sugar 3. 54g; Protein 9. 18g

Cheesy Veggie Omelet

Prep Time: 10 minutes | Cook Time: 10 minutes | Serves: 1

2 large eggs
¼ cup milk
½ cup shredded cheddar cheese
2 tablespoons diced mushrooms
2 tablespoons diced red bell pepper

1 tablespoon diced scallions, white and pale green parts, plus deep green parts for garnish
Salt
Freshly ground black pepper
Extra-virgin olive oil

1. Whisk together the eggs and milk in a medium bowl. 2. Add the cheese, bell pepper, mushrooms, and diced scallions to stir. Add salt and black pepper. 3. Generously spray the crisper plate with oil. 4. Install the crisper plate in both baskets, place the egg mixture in the baskets, and insert the baskets into the unit. 5. Select Zone 1 and select AIR FRY. Then set the temperature to 350°F and set the time to 6 minutes. Select MATCH COOK to match the Settings in Zone 2 with those in Zone 1. Select START/PAUSE to begin. 6. Cook for 6 minutes, then start checking the omelet every minute until the eggs are set. When it is fully cooked, usually 6 to 8 minutes, a toothpick inserted in the middle should come out clean. 7. Once cooking has finished, carefully slide the omelet onto a plate. Serve flat, garnished with sliced scallions, if using.

Per Serving: Calories 446; Fat 35. 49g; Sodium 1634mg; Carbs 7. 77g; Fiber 1. 1g; Sugar 4. 43g; Protein 23. 86g

Cheesy Tomato Frittata

Prep Time: 10 minutes | Cook Time: 10 minutes | Serves: 2

Extra-virgin olive oil, for the pan
4 large eggs
3 tablespoons heavy (whipping) cream
2 tablespoons chopped fresh basil
¾ cup shredded mozzarella cheese

⅓ cup oil-packed sun-dried tomatoes, patted dry and chopped fine
Salt
Freshly ground black pepper

1. Generously spray the crisper plate with oil. 2. In a medium bowl, whisk together the eggs and cream. Add the basil, sun-dried tomatoes, salt, cheese, and pepper and stir. 3. Install the crisper plate in both baskets, place the egg mixture in the baskets, and insert the baskets into the unit. 4. Select Zone 1 and select AIR FRY. Then set the temperature to 350°F and set the time to 10 minutes. Select MATCH COOK to match the Settings in Zone 2 with those in Zone 1. Select START/PAUSE to begin. 5. Cook for 10 to 12 minutes until the top is golden and a toothpick inserted in the middle comes out clean. 6. Once cooking has finished, serve.

Per Serving: Calories 297; Fat 20. 94g; Sodium 970mg; Carbs 8. 02g; Fiber 2g; Sugar 1. 46g; Protein 20. 36g

Cheesy Ham Breakfast Pockets

Prep Time: 10 minutes | Cook Time: 10 minutes | Serves: 4

2 (8-ounce) cans crescent rolls, refrigerated
8 tablespoons shredded cheddar cheese, divided

4 tablespoons diced cooked ham, divided
Extra-virgin olive oil, for spraying

1. Open the crescent roll tubes and unroll each crescent triangle. You should have 16 triangles. 2. Place 1 tablespoon cheese and ½ tablespoon ham in the center of 8 crescent triangles. 3. Place the remaining 8 crescent triangles on top each filled triangle and press all the edges together to seal the toppings inside the pocket. 4. Lightly spray the crisper plate with oil. 5. Install the crisper plate in both baskets, place the breakfast pockets in a single layer in the baskets, not overcrowd. Lightly spray with oil and insert the baskets into the unit. 6. Select Zone 1 and select AIR FRY. Then set the temperature to 350°F and set the time to 5 minutes. Select MATCH COOK to match the Settings in Zone 2 with those in Zone 1. Select START/PAUSE to begin. 7. Cook for 5 minutes. Flip the pockets and lightly spray with oil. Cook for another 3 to 5 minutes until the crescent dough is fully cooked and the tops are golden brown. 8. Once cooking has finished, serve.

Per Serving: Calories 140; Fat 6. 24g; Sodium 366mg; Carbs 12. 15g; Fiber 0. 4g; Sugar 1. 37g; Protein 8. 66g

Chapter 2 Vegetables and Sides

Cheesy Beet & Spinach Salad

Prep Time: 10 minutes | Cook Time: 65 minutes | Serves: 4

¾ cup of crumbled feta cheese
2 cups mixed baby spinach
½ teaspoon thyme leaves, minced
1 teaspoon marjoram, fresh, minced
1 teaspoon parsley, fresh, minced
½ tablespoon liquid Stevia
1½ teaspoons Dijon mustard

2 cloves of minced garlic
¼ cup red onion, minced
3 tablespoons red wine vinegar
Salt and pepper to taste
2 tablespoons olive oil
7 large beets, stems trimmed
Pistachios for garnishing

1. Wash the beets and dry them. Place the beets on piece of aluminum foil. 2. Install the crisper plate in both baskets, put the beets in the baskets, drizzling with the oil, and insert the baskets into the unit. 3. Select Zone 1 and select BAKE. Then set the temperature to 390°F and set the time to 20 minutes. Select MATCH COOK to match the Settings in Zone 2 with those in Zone 1. Then select START/PAUSE to begin. 4. Season with the pepper and salt and cook for an additional 45 minutes. 5. Once cooking has finished, remove them and place in fridge. 6. In a mixing bowl, combine garlic, onion, stevia, and mustard. Whisk these ingredients until they are well blended. Add the herbs to stir and season with salt and pepper. 7. When the beets are chilled, cut them into half-inch slices. Garnish with lettuce and pistachios.
Per Serving: Calories 225; Fat 14. 47g; Sodium 986mg; Carbs 17. 86g; Fiber 5g; Sugar 11. 47g; Protein 7. 51g

Crispy Onion Pakora

Prep Time: 10 minutes | Cook Time: 6 minutes | Serves: 6

1 cup graham flour
¼ teaspoon turmeric powder
Salt to taste
⅛ teaspoon chili powder
¼ teaspoon carom

1 tablespoon fresh coriander, chopped
2 green chili peppers, finely chopped
4 onions, finely chopped
2 teaspoons vegetable oil
¼ cup rice flour

1. Combine the flours and oil in a mixing bowl. Add water as needed to create a dough-like consistency. Add the onions, peppers, coriander, chili powder, carom, and turmeric. 2. Roll vegetable mixture into small balls. Install the crisper plate in the basket, put the small balls in the basket, and insert the basket into the unit. 3. Select Zone 1 and select AIR FRY. Then set the temperature to 350°F and set the time to 6 minutes. Select START/PAUSE to begin. 4. Once cooking has finished, serve with hot sauce!
Per Serving: Calories 190; Fat 2. 11g; Sodium 409mg; Carbs 39. 14g; Fiber 3. 1g; Sugar 11. 97g; Protein 4. 72g

Lemony Charred Shishito Peppers

Prep Time: 10 minutes | Cook Time: 5 minutes | Serves: 4

20 Shishito peppers
1 teaspoon vegetable oil

Sea salt to taste
1 lemon, juiced

1. Toss Shishito peppers with salt and oil. Brush the crisper plate with oil. Install the crisper plate in both baskets, put the peppers in the baskets, and insert the baskets into the unit. 2. Select Zone 1 and select AIR FRY. Then set the temperature to 390°F and set the time to 5 minutes. Select MATCH COOK to match the Settings in Zone 2 with those in Zone 1. Then select START/PAUSE to begin. 3. Once cooking has finished, transfer the peppers to bowl. Squeeze the lemon juice over peppers and season with coarse sea salt. Serve as finger food.
Per Serving: Calories 103; Fat 1. 6g; Sodium 597mg; Carbs 22. 11g; Fiber 3. 4g; Sugar 11. 78g; Protein 4. 54g

Tasty Semolina Veggie Cutlets
Prep Time: 10 minutes | Cook Time: 23 minutes | Serves: 4

1 cup semolina
Olive oil for frying
Salt and pepper to taste

1½ cups of your favorite veggies(suggestion: carrot, peas, green beans, bell pepper and cauliflower)
5 cups milk

1. Stir and warm the milk in a saucepan over medium heat. Add vegetables when it becomes hot and cook until they are softened for about 3 minutes. Season with salt and pepper. 2. Add the semolina to milk mixture and cook for another 10 minutes. 3. Remove from heat and spread thin across a piece of parchment on a baking sheet. Chill for 4 hours in the fridge. 4. Take out the baking sheet from the fridge, cut semolina mixture into cutlets. 5. Brush the cutlets with oil. Install the crisper plate in the basket, put the cutlets in the basket, and insert the basket into the unit. 6. Select Zone 1 and select BAKE. Then set the temperature to 350°F and set the time to 10 minutes. Select START/PAUSE to begin. 7. Once cooking has finished, serve with hot sauce!
Per Serving: Calories 373; Fat 11. 69g; Sodium 731mg; Carbs 50. 34g; Fiber 3. 9g; Sugar 17. 05g; Protein 15. 92g

Cheesy Green Bean Casserole
Time: 10 minutes | Cook Time: 15 minutes | Serves: 4

4 tablespoons unsalted butter
¼ cup diced yellow onion
½ cup chopped white mushrooms
½ cup heavy whipping cream
1 ounce full-fat cream cheese

½ cup chicken broth
¼ teaspoon xanthan gum
1 pound fresh green beans, edges trimmed
½ ounce pork rinds, finely ground

1. In a medium skillet over medium heat, melt the butter. Sauté the onion and mushrooms for about 3 to 5 minutes until they become soft and fragrant. 2. Add the cream cheese, heavy whipping cream, and broth to the pan. Whisk until smooth. Bring to a boil and then reduce to a simmer. Sprinkle the xanthan gum into the pan and remove from heat. 3. Chop the green beans into 2" pieces. Install the crisper plate in both baskets, place the green beans in the baskets. Pour the sauce mixture over them and stir until coated. Top the dish with ground pork rinds. Insert the baskets into the unit. 4. Select Zone 1 and select AIR FRY. Then set the temperature to 320°F and set the time to 15 minutes. Select MATCH COOK to match the Settings in Zone 2 with those in Zone 1. Select START/PAUSE to begin. 5. Once cooking has finished, top will be golden and green beans fork tender when fully cooked. Serve warm.
Per Serving: Calories 229; Fat 17. 84g; Sodium 168mg; Carbs 7. 91g; Fiber 3. 3g; Sugar 2. 19g; Protein 10. 64g

Garlic Asparagus
Prep Time: 10 minutes | Cook Time: 10 minutes | Serves: 4

10 asparagus spears, woody ends chopped off
Salt and pepper to taste

1 garlic clove, minced
4 tablespoons olive oil

1. Combine the oil and garlic in a bowl. 2. Coat the asparagus with oil mixture. Install the crisper plate in both baskets, put the asparagus in the baskets, and insert the baskets into the unit. 3. Select Zone 1 and select AIR FRY. Then set the temperature to 400°F and set the time to 5 minutes. Select MATCH COOK to match the Settings in Zone 2 with those in Zone 1. Then select START/PAUSE to begin. 4. Season the asparagus with the salt and pepper and cook for 10 minutes. 5. Once cooking has finished, serve.
Per Serving: Calories 124; Fat 13. 53g; Sodium 582mg; Carbs 0. 96g; Fiber 0. 3g; Sugar 0. 18g; Protein 0. 3g

Lime Chili Cauliflower

Prep Time: 10 minutes | Cook Time: 7 minutes | Serves: 4

2 cups chopped cauliflower florets	½ teaspoon garlic powder
2 tablespoons coconut oil, melted	1 medium lime
2 teaspoons chili powder	2 tablespoons chopped cilantro

1. In a large bowl, mix cauliflower with coconut oil. Sprinkle with chili powder and garlic powder. Install the crisper plate in the basket, place the seasoned cauliflower in the basket, and insert the basket into the unit. 2. Select Zone 1 and select AIR FRY. Then set the temperature to 350°F and set the time to 7 minutes. Select START/PAUSE to begin. 3. Cauliflower will be tender and begin to turn golden at the edges. Once cooking has finished, place into serving bowl. 4. Cut the lime into quarters and squeeze juice over cauliflower. Garnish with cilantro.

Per Serving: Calories 80; Fat 7. 16g; Sodium 55mg; Carbs 4. 57g; Fiber 1. 6g; Sugar 1. 32g; Protein 1. 33g

Herbed Butter Radishes

Prep Time: 10 minutes | Cook Time: 10 minutes | Serves: 4

1 pound radishes	½ teaspoon dried parsley
2 tablespoons unsalted butter, melted	¼ teaspoon dried oregano
½ teaspoon garlic powder	¼ teaspoon ground black pepper

1. Remove roots from radishes and cut into quarters. 2. Add butter and seasonings in a small bowl. Toss the radishes in the herb butter. Install the crisper plate in both baskets, place the radishes in the baskets, and insert the baskets into the unit. 3. Select Zone 1 and select AIR FRY. Then set the temperature to 350°F and set the time to 10 minutes. Select MATCH COOK to match the Settings in Zone 2 with those in Zone 1. Select START/PAUSE to begin. 4. Halfway through the cooking time, toss the radishes in the basket. Continue cooking until edges begin to turn brown. 5. Once cooking has finished, serve warm.

Per Serving: Calories 58; Fat 3. 98g; Sodium 27mg; Carbs 5. 27g; Fiber 1. 9g; Sugar 2. 99g; Protein 1. 05g

Cheesy Sausage–Stuffed Mushroom Caps

Prep Time: 10 minutes | Cook Time: 8 minutes | Serves: 2

6 large portobello mushroom caps	2 tablespoons blanched finely ground almond flour
½ pound Italian sausage	¼ cup grated Parmesan cheese
¼ cup chopped onion	1 teaspoon minced fresh garlic

1. Use a spoon to hollow out each mushroom cap, reserving scrapings. 2. In a medium skillet, cook the sausage over medium heat for about 10 minutes until fully cooked and no pink remains. Drain and then add Parmesan, almond flour, onion, reserved mushroom scrapings, and garlic. Gently fold ingredients together and continue cooking another minute, then remove from heat. 3. Evenly spoon the mixture into mushroom caps. Install the crisper plate in both baskets, place the caps in the baskets, and insert the baskets into the unit. 4. Select Zone 1 and select AIR FRY. Then set the temperature to 375°F and set the time to 8 minutes. Select MATCH COOK to match the Settings in Zone 2 with those in Zone 1. Select START/PAUSE to begin. 5. When finished cooking, the tops will be browned and bubbling. Serve warm.

Per Serving: Calories 531; Fat 44. 3g; Sodium 1066mg; Carbs 9. 76g; Fiber 3g; Sugar 2. 98g; Protein 24. 7g

Spicy–Sweet Brussels Sprouts

Prep Time: 15 minutes | Cook Time: 20 minutes | Serves: 2

¼ cup Thai sweet chili sauce
2 tablespoons black vinegar or balsamic vinegar
½ teaspoon hot sauce, such as Tabasco
8 ounces Brussels sprouts, trimmed (large sprouts halved)

2 small shallots, cut into ¼-inch-thick slices
Kosher salt and freshly ground black pepper
2 teaspoons lightly packed fresh cilantro leaves

1. In a large bowl, whisk together the vinegar, chili sauce, and hot sauce. Add the Brussels sprouts and shallots and season with salt and pepper. Toss to combine. 2. Install the crisper plate in both baskets, place the Brussels sprouts and sauce in the baskets, and insert the baskets into the unit. 3. Select Zone 1 and select AIR FRY. Then set the temperature to 375°F and set the time to 20 minutes. Select MATCH COOK to match the Settings in Zone 2 with those in Zone 1. Select START/PAUSE to begin. Stir every 5 minutes until the Brussels sprouts are tender and the sauce is reduced to a sticky glaze. 4. Once cooking has finished, remove and transfer the Brussels sprouts to plates. Sprinkle with the cilantro and serve warm.

Per Serving: Calories 96; Fat 0. 48g; Sodium 1101mg; Carbs 19. 14g; Fiber 6. 8g; Sugar 6. 96g; Protein 5. 01g

Buttered Potato, Cauliflower and Pea Turnovers

Time: 15 minutes | Cook Time: 20 minutes | Serves: 4

Dough:
2 cups all-purpose flour
½ teaspoon baking powder
1 teaspoon salt
Freshly ground black pepper

¼ teaspoon dried thyme
¼ cup canola oil
½ to ⅔ cup water

Turnover Filling:
1 tablespoon canola or vegetable oil
1 onion, finely chopped
1 clove garlic, minced
1 tablespoon grated fresh ginger
½ teaspoon cumin seeds
½ teaspoon fennel seeds
1 teaspoon curry powder

2 russet potatoes, diced
2 cups cauliflower florets
½ cup frozen peas
2 tablespoons chopped fresh cilantro
Salt and freshly ground black pepper
2 tablespoons butter, melted
Mango chutney, for serving

1. Start by making the dough. Combine the flour, salt, pepper, baking powder, and dried thyme in a mixing bowl or the bowl of a stand mixer. Drizzle in the canola oil and pinch it together with your fingers to turn the flour into a crumby mixture. Stir in the water (enough to bring the dough together). Knead the dough for 5 minutes or so until it is smooth. Add a little more water or flour as needed. Let the dough rest while you make the turnover filling. 2. Pre-heat a large skillet on the stovetop over medium-high heat. Add the oil and sauté the onion until it starts to become tender – about 4 minutes. Add the ginger and garlic to cook for another minute. Add the dried spices and toss everything to coat. Add the potatoes and cauliflower to the skillet and pour in 1½ cups of water. Simmer everything together for 20 to 25 minutes, or until the potatoes are soft and most of the water has evaporated. If the water has evaporated and the vegetables still need more time, just add a little water and continue to simmer until everything is tender. Stir well, crushing the potatoes and cauliflower a little as you do so. Stir in the peas and cilantro, season with freshly ground black pepper and salt. Then set aside to cool. 3. Divide the dough into 4 balls. Roll the dough balls out into ¼-inch thick circles. Divide the cooled potato filling between the dough circles, placing a mound of the filling on one side of each piece of dough, letting leave an empty border around the edge of the dough. Brush the edges of the dough with a little water and fold one edge of circle over the filling to meet the other edge of the circle, creating a half moon. Pinch the edges together with your fingers. Then using the tines of a fork to press the edge to decorate and seal. 4. Spray or brush the crisper plate with oil. 5. Install the crisper plate in both baskets. Brush the turnovers with the melted butter, place the 4 turnovers in the baskets, and insert the baskets into the unit. 6. Select Zone 1 and select AIR FRY. Then set the temperature to 380°F and set the time to 15 minutes. Select MATCH COOK to match the Settings in Zone 2 with those in Zone 1. Select START/PAUSE to begin. Cook for 15 minutes. Flip the turnovers over and cook for another 5 minutes. 7. Once cooking has finished, these will be very hot when they come out of the air fryer. Let them cool for at least 20 minutes before serving warm with mango chutney.

Per Serving: Calories 633; Fat 24. 14g; Sodium 1244mg; Carbs 93. 54g; Fiber 7. 1g; Sugar 7. 07g; Protein 13g

Delicious Cheesy Cauliflower Tots
Time: 15 minutes | Cook Time: 2 minutes | Serves: 4

1 large head cauliflower
1 cup shredded mozzarella cheese
½ cup grated Parmesan cheese
1 large egg

¼ teaspoon garlic powder
¼ teaspoon dried parsley
⅛ teaspoon onion powder

1. Place a large pot with 2 cups water on the stovetop and place a steamer in the pan. Bring water to a boil. Cut the cauliflower into florets and put on steamer basket. Cover the pot with the lid. 2. Allow cauliflower to cook 7 minutes until fork tender. Remove and place into cheesecloth or clean kitchen towel to let cool. Squeeze over sink to remove excess moisture as much as possible. The mixture will be too soft to form into tots if not all the moisture is removed. Mash to a smooth consistency with a fork. 3. Place the cauliflower into a large mixing bowl and add mozzarella, egg, Parmesan, parsley, garlic powder, and onion powder. Stir until fully combined. The mixture should be wet but easy to mold. 4. Take 2 tablespoons of the mixture and roll into tot shape. Repeat with remaining mixture. 5. Install the crisper plate in both baskets, place the mixture in the baskets, and insert the baskets into the unit. Select Zone 1 and select AIR FRY. Then set the temperature to 320°F and set the time to 12 minutes. Select MATCH COOK to match the Settings in Zone 2 with those in Zone 1. Select START/PAUSE to begin. 6. Turn tots halfway through the cooking time. Cauliflower tots should be golden when fully cooked. 7. Once cooking has finished, serve warm.
Per Serving: Calories 124; Fat 4. 8g; Sodium 458mg; Carbs 6. 38g; Fiber 1. 9g; Sugar 1. 73g; Protein 14. 5g

Savory Samosas
Prep Time: 10 minutes | Cook Time: 20 minutes | Serves: 4

2 cups all-purpose flour
½ teaspoon cumin seeds
2 tablespoons olive oil
1 teaspoon turmeric
1 teaspoon chili powder
1 teaspoon ginger-garlic paste

2 teaspoons garam masala powder
½ cup green peas
2 russet potatoes, peeled and cubed
1 teaspoon carom seeds
2 teaspoons ghee butter

1. Prepare the crust in a bowl, combining the flour, carom seeds, water as needed to make a dough. 2. Knead dough and chill in the fridge for 30 minutes. 3. Prepare the filling: Cover the potatoes with water in a saucepan and bring to a boil. Add peas and continue to boil until vegetables are tender. Drain and mash well. 4. Add the garam masala, chili powder, ginger-garlic paste, and turmeric to potato mixture. Season with salt and mix well. 5. In a small pan, sauté the oil over medium heat. Add the cumin seeds and toast they are sizzling and aromatic. Add the cumin to potato mixture, mix well, then set aside. 6. Retrieve the dough out of the fridge, roll it out on the counter, and cut into several squares about 4-inches across. 7. Place a spoonful of filling in each square and fold samosa to a triangle-like shape, carefully sealing edges. 8. Brush the samosas with oil. Install the crisper plate in both baskets, put the samosas in the baskets, and insert the baskets into the unit. 9. Select Zone 1 and select AIR FRY. Then set the temperature to 350°F and set the time to 20 minutes. Select MATCH COOK to match the Settings in Zone 2 with those in Zone 1. Then select START/PAUSE to begin. Cook them until they are golden brown. 10. Once cooking has finished, serve warm or cold.
Per Serving: Calories 413; Fat 10. 11g; Sodium 102mg; Carbs 70. 62g; Fiber 4. 7g; Sugar 1. 59g; Protein 10. 11g

Garlic Vegetable Spring Rolls

Prep Time: 10 minutes | Cook Time: 23 minutes | Serves: 10

10 spring roll wrappers
2 tablespoons cornstarch
Water
3 green onions, thinly sliced
1 tablespoon black pepper
1 teaspoon soy sauce
Pinches of salt

2 tablespoons cooking oil, plus more for brushing
8-cloves of garlic, minced
½ bell pepper, cut into thin matchsticks
2 large onions, cut into thin matchsticks
1 large carrot, cut into thin matchsticks
2 cups cabbage, shredded
2-inch piece of ginger, grated

1. To prepare the filling: add the carrot, onion, bell pepper, cabbage, ginger, and garlic in a large bowl. 2. Gently add two tablespoons of olive oil in a pan over high heat. Add the filling mixture and stir in salt and a dash of stevia sweetener if you like. Cook for 3 minutes. Add soy sauce, black pepper and mix well. 3. Add the green onions, stir and set aside. 4. In a small bowl, combine enough water and cornstarch to make a creamy paste. 5. Fill the rolls with a tablespoon of filling in center of each wrapper and roll tightly, dampening the edges with cornstarch paste to ensure a good seal. Repeat until all wrappers and filling are used. 6. Brush the rolls with oil. Install the crisper plate in both baskets, put the rolls in the baskets, and insert the baskets into the unit. 7. Select Zone 1 and select AIR FRY. Then set the temperature to 350°F and set the time to 20 minutes. Select MATCH COOK to match the Settings in Zone 2 with those in Zone 1. Then select START/PAUSE to begin. 8. Cook them until crisp and golden. Halfway through the cook time flip them over. 9. Once cooking has finished, serve.
Per Serving: Calories 153; Fat 3. 43g; Sodium 437mg; Carbs 26. 66g; Fiber 2g; Sugar 2. 69g; Protein 4. 14g

Homemade Potato Tots

Prep Time: 10 minutes | Cook Time: 8 minutes | Serves: 2

1 large potato, diced
Salt and pepper to taste

1 teaspoon onion, minced
1 tablespoon olive oil

1. In a saucepan, cover the potatoes with water and boil over medium-high heat. Drain the potatoes and place in a bowl and mash potatoes. 2. Add the olive oil, pepper, onion, and salt to mashed potatoes and mix well. Make the small tots from potato mixture. 3. Install the crisper plate in the basket, put the small tots in the basket, and insert the basket into the unit. 4. Select Zone 1 and select AIR FRY. Then set the temperature to 380°F and set the time to 8 minutes. Select START/PAUSE to begin. 5. Shake the basket and cook for another 5 minutes. 6. Once cooking has finished, serve hot!
Per Serving: Calories 225; Fat 6. 99g; Sodium 595mg; Carbs 37. 75g; Fiber 5. 1g; Sugar 3. 77g; Protein 4. 39g

Easy Potatoes

Prep Time: 10 minutes | Cook Time: 20 minutes | Serves: 4

4 potatoes
Salt and pepper to taste

Olive oil as needed

1. Peel the potatoes and then cut them in half. 2. Brush the potatoes gently with oil. Install the crisper plate in both baskets, put the potatoes in the baskets, and insert the baskets into the unit. 3. Select Zone 1 and select AIR FRY. Then set the temperature to 355°F and set the time to 10 minutes. Select MATCH COOK to match the Settings in Zone 2 with those in Zone 1. Then select START/PAUSE to begin. 4. Brush again with oil and cook for another 10 minutes. 5. Once cooking has finished, serve.
Per Serving: Calories 178; Fat 1. 31g; Sodium 595mg; Carbs 38. 29g; Fiber 4. 9g; Sugar 2. 24g; Protein 4. 53g

Cheesy Zucchini Chips

Prep Time: 10 minutes | Cook Time: 10 minutes | Serves: 4

2 medium zucchini
1 ounce pork rinds

½ cup grated Parmesan cheese
1 large egg

1. Slice zucchini in ¼-thick slices. Arrange between a clean kitchen towel or two layers of paper towels to remove excess moisture for 30 minutes. 2. Put pork rinds into food processor and pulse until finely ground. Place in into medium bowl to mix with Parmesan. 3. Beat egg in a small bowl. 4. Dip zucchini slices in egg and then in pork rind mixture, coating as completely as possible. Install the crisper plate in both baskets, place each slice in a single layer in the baskets, and insert the baskets into the unit. 5. Select Zone 1 and select AIR FRY. Then set the temperature to 320°F and set the time to 10 minutes. Select MATCH COOK to match the Settings in Zone 2 with those in Zone 1. Select START/PAUSE to begin. 6. Flip chips halfway through the cooking time. 7. Once cooking has finished, serve warm.

Per Serving: Calories 82; Fat 5. 3g; Sodium 232mg; Carbs 2. 06g; Fiber 0. 1g; Sugar 0. 03g; Protein 6. 35g

Easy Roasted Garlic

Prep Time: 5 minutes | Cook Time: 20 minutes | Serves: 12

1 medium head garlic

2 teaspoons avocado oil

1. Remove any hanging excess peel from the garlic but leave the cloves covered. Cut off ¼ of the head of garlic, exposing the tips of the cloves. 2. Drizzle with avocado oil. Place the garlic head into a small sheet of aluminum foil, completely enclosing it. Install the crisper plate in the basket, place the garlic in the basket, and insert the basket into the unit. 3. Select Zone 1 and select AIR FRY. Then set the temperature to 400°F and set the time to 20 minutes. Select START/PAUSE to begin. If your garlic head is a bit smaller, check it after 15 minutes. 4. When done, garlic should be golden brown and very soft. 5. To serve, cloves should pop out and easily be spread or sliced. Place in an airtight container and store in the refrigerator for 5 days. You may also freeze individual cloves on a baking sheet, then store together in a freezer-safe storage bag once frozen.

Per Serving: Calories 24; Fat 0. 81g; Sodium 2mg; Carbs 3. 75g; Fiber 0. 2g; Sugar 0. 11g; Protein 0. 72g

Cheesy Coconut Biscuits

Prep Time: 10 minutes | Cook Time: 12 minutes | Serves: 4

⅓ cup coconut flour
½ teaspoon baking powder
½ teaspoon garlic powder
1 large egg

¼ cup unsalted butter, melted and divided
½ cup shredded sharp Cheddar cheese
1 scallion, sliced

1. Mix baking powder, coconut flour, with garlic powder in a large bowl. 2. Stir in egg, half of the melted butter, Cheddar cheese, and scallions. Install the crisper plate in the basket, place the mixture in the basket, and insert the basket into the unit. 3. Select Zone 1 and select AIR FRY. Then set the temperature to 320°F and set the time to 12 minutes. Select START/PAUSE to begin. 4. Once cooking has finished, to serve, remove and allow to fully cool. Slice into four pieces and pour remaining melted butter over each.

Per Serving: Calories 157; Fat 14. 47g; Sodium 136mg; Carbs 1. 97g; Fiber 0. 4g; Sugar 0. 68g; Protein 5. 38g

Buttered Pumpkin Seed Brown Bread

Prep Time: 10 minutes | Cook Time: 28 minutes | Serves: 4

8 ounces of almond flour
1 ounce of liquid Stevia
1 egg

2 tablespoons butter
½ cup pumpkin seeds

1. Mix all the ingredients in a bowl, except the butter and egg. Keep mixing with hands. 2. Add the butter and knead mixture. Let the bread dough rest, keep it covered and warm for about 2 hours or until it doubles in size. 3. Once this happens, divide the dough into small balls of about 1-ounce each and place in a baking paper. Top with pumpkin seeds. Brush the balls with the egg and allow dough to rest for 40 minutes. 4. Install the crisper plate in both baskets, put the dough balls in the baskets, and insert the baskets into the unit. 5. Select Zone 1 and select AIR FRY. Then set the temperature to 330°F and set the time to 20 minutes. Select MATCH COOK to match the Settings in Zone 2 with those in Zone 1. Then select START/PAUSE to begin. Cook until brown and cooked. 6. Once cooking has finished, serve.
Per Serving: Calories 497; Fat 43. 71g; Sodium 110mg; Carbs 14. 8g; Fiber 8. 2g; Sugar 2. 82g; Protein 18. 7g

Classic Dinner Rolls

Prep Time: 10 minutes | Cook Time: 12 minutes | Serves: 6

1 cup shredded mozzarella cheese
1 ounce full-fat cream cheese
1 cup blanched finely ground almond flour

¼ cup ground flaxseed
½ teaspoon baking powder
1 large egg

1. Place cream cheese, mozzarella, and almond flour in a large microwave-safe bowl. Microwave for 1 minute. Mix until smooth. 2. Add flaxseed, baking powder, and egg until fully combined and smooth. Microwave another 15 seconds if it becomes too firm. 3. Divide the dough into six pieces and roll into balls. Install the crisper plate in the basket, place the balls in the basket, and insert the basket into the unit. 4. Select Zone 1 and select AIR FRY. Then set the temperature to 320°F and set the time to 12 minutes. Select START/PAUSE to begin. 5. Once cooking has finished, allow rolls to cool completely before serving.
Per Serving: Calories 226; Fat 17. 12g; Sodium 165mg; Carbs 7. 87g; Fiber 4. 7g; Sugar 1. 8g; Protein 13. 24g

Homemade Flatbread

Prep Time: 5 minutes | Cook Time: 7 minutes | Serves: 2

1 cup shredded mozzarella cheese
¼ cup blanched finely ground almond flour

1 ounce full-fat cream cheese, softened

1. In a large microwave-safe bowl, melt mozzarella in the microwave for 30 seconds. Stir in almond flour until smooth and then add cream cheese. Continue mixing until dough forms, gently kneading it with wet hands if necessary. 2. Separate the dough into two pieces and roll out to ¼" thickness between two pieces of parchment. Cut another piece of parchment to fit the basket. 3. Place a piece of flatbread onto your parchment. Install the crisper plate in both baskets, place the flatbread in the baskets, and insert the baskets into the unit. 4. Select Zone 1 and select AIR FRY. Then set the temperature to 320°F and set the time to 7 minutes. Select MATCH COOK to match the Settings in Zone 2 with those in Zone 1. Select START/PAUSE to begin. 5. Flip the flatbread halfway through the cooking time. 6. Once cooking has finished, serve warm.
Per Serving: Calories 215; Fat 11. 7g; Sodium 474mg; Carbs 6. 52g; Fiber 2. 8g; Sugar 2. 5g; Protein 22. 91g

Cheesy Asparagus & Mushroom Soufflés
Prep Time: 15 minutes | Cook Time: 21 minutes | Serves: 3

Butter
Grated Parmesan cheese
3 button mushrooms, thinly sliced
8 spears asparagus, sliced ½-inch long
1 teaspoon olive oil
1 tablespoon butter
4½ teaspoons flour

Pinch paprika
Pinch ground nutmeg
Salt and freshly ground black pepper
½ cup milk
½ cup grated Gruyère cheese or other Swiss cheese (about 2 ounces)
2 eggs, separated

1. Butter three 6-ounce ramekins and dust with grated Parmesan cheese. 2. Toss the mushrooms and asparagus in a bowl with the olive oil. 3. Install the crisper plate in the basket, place the vegetables in the basket, and insert the basket into the unit. Select Zone 1 and select AIR FRY. Then set the temperature to 400°F and set the time to 7 minutes. Select START/PAUSE to begin. Shake the basket once or twice to make the ingredients redistribution while they cook. 4. While the vegetables are cooking, make the soufflé base. Cook the butter to melt in a saucepan on the stovetop over medium heat. Add the flour to stir and cook for a minute or two. Add the paprika, salt, nutmeg, and pepper. Add the milk and bring the mixture to a simmer to thicken. Once cooking has finished, remove and add the cheese, stirring to melt. Let the mixture cool for just a few minutes and then whisk the egg yolks in, one at a time. Stir in the cooked mushrooms and asparagus. Let this soufflé base cool. 5. In a separate bowl, whisk the egg whites to soft peak stage (the point at which the whites can almost stand up on the end of your whisk). Fold the whipped egg whites into the soufflé base, adding a little at a time. 6. Then set the temperature to 330°F. 7. Transfer the batter carefully to the buttered ramekins, leaving about ½-inch at the top. Place the ramekins into the basket and cook for 14 minutes. The soufflés should have risen nicely and be brown on top. Serve immediately.
Per Serving: Calories 295; Fat 22. 5g; Sodium 479mg; Carbs 9. 98g; Fiber 1g; Sugar 2. 92g; Protein 13. 57g

Mole–Braised Chili Cauliflower
Prep Time: 15 minutes | Cook Time: 20 minutes | Serves: 2

8 ounces medium cauliflower florets
1 tablespoon vegetable oil
Kosher salt and freshly ground black pepper
1½ cups vegetable broth
2 tablespoons New Mexico chile powder (or regular chili powder)
2 tablespoons salted roasted peanuts

1 tablespoon toasted sesame seeds, plus more for garnish
1 tablespoon finely chopped golden raisins
1 teaspoon kosher salt
1 teaspoon dark brown sugar
½ teaspoon dried oregano
¼ teaspoon cayenne pepper
⅛ teaspoon ground cinnamon

1. Mix the cauliflower with the oil and season with black pepper and salt in a large bowl. 2. Install the crisper plate in both baskets, place the cauliflower in the baskets, and insert the baskets into the unit. 3. Select Zone 1 and select AIR FRY. Then set the temperature to 375°F and set the time to 10 minutes. Select MATCH COOK to match the Settings in Zone 2 with those in Zone 1. Select START/PAUSE to begin. Cook until tender and lightly browned at the edges, and stir halfway through. 4. Meanwhile, in a small blender, add the broth, chilies powder, salt, sesame seeds, peanuts, raisins, brown sugar, cayenne, oregano, and cinnamon and puree until smooth. Pour into a small saucepan or skillet and bring to a simmer over medium heat. Cook for 3 to 5 minutes until reduced by half. 5. Pour the hot mole sauce over the cauliflower in the basket, stir to coat, then cook until the sauce is thickened and lightly charred on the cauliflower, about 5 minutes more. 6. Once cooking has finished, sprinkle with more sesame seeds and serve warm.
Per Serving: Calories 286; Fat 18. 3g; Sodium 1942mg; Carbs 29. 33g; Fiber 7. 9g; Sugar 15. 28g; Protein 8. 29g

Creamy Pesto Potato

Prep Time: 15 minutes | Cook Time: 40 minutes | Serves: 2

2 medium russet potatoes (8 to 10 ounces each)
5 tablespoons olive oil
Kosher salt and freshly ground black pepper
¼ cup roughly chopped fresh chives
2 tablespoons packed fresh flat-leaf parsley leaves

1 tablespoon chopped walnuts
1 tablespoon grated parmesan cheese
1 teaspoon fresh lemon juice
1 small garlic clove, peeled
¼ cup sour cream

1. Place the potatoes on a cutting board and lay a chopstick or thin-handled wooden spoon to the side of each potato. Thinly slice the potatoes crosswise, letting the chopstick or spoon handle stop the blade of your knife, and stop ½ inch short of each end of the potato. Rub the potatoes with 1 tablespoon of the olive oil and season with salt and pepper. 2. Install the crisper plate in the basket, place the potatoes, cut-side up, in the basket, and insert the basket into the unit. 3. Select Zone 1 and select AIR FRY. Then set the temperature to 375°F and set the time to 40 minutes. Select START/PAUSE to begin. Cook until golden brown and crisp on the outside and tender inside, drizzling the insides with 1 tablespoon more olive oil and seasoning with more salt and pepper halfway through. 4. Meanwhile, combine the remaining 3 tablespoons olive oil, the chives, lemon juice, walnuts, parsley, parmesan, and garlic and puree in a small blender or food processor until smooth. Season the chive pesto with salt and pepper. 5. Once cooking has finished, remove the potatoes and transfer to plates. Drizzle the potatoes with the pesto, letting it drip down into the grooves, then dollop each with sour cream and serve hot.
Per Serving: Calories 546; Fat 40. 04g; Sodium 664mg; Carbs 42. 55g; Fiber 3. 4g; Sugar 1. 55g; Protein 7. 5g

Caesar Cheesy Whole Cauliflower

Prep Time: 15 minutes | Cook Time: 40 minutes | Serves: 2-4

3 tablespoons olive oil
2 tablespoons red wine vinegar
2 tablespoons Worcestershire sauce
2 tablespoons grated parmesan cheese
1 tablespoon Dijon mustard
4 garlic cloves, minced
4 oil-packed anchovy fillets, drained and finely minced

Kosher salt and freshly ground black pepper
1 small head cauliflower (about 1 pound), green leaves trimmed and stem trimmed flush with the bottom of the head
1 tablespoon roughly chopped fresh flat-leaf parsley (optional)

1. Whisk together the olive oil, Worcestershire, vinegar, parmesan, mustard, anchovies, garlic, salt, and pepper in a liquid measuring cup. Place the cauliflower head upside down on a cutting board and use a paring knife to make an "x" through the full length of the core. Transfer the cauliflower head to a large bowl and pour half the dressing over it. Turn the cauliflower head to coat it in the dressing, then let it rest, stem-side up, in the dressing for at least 10 minutes and up to 30 minutes to allow the dressing to seep into all its nooks and crannies. 2. Install the crisper plate in the basket, place the cauliflower head in the basket, stem-side down. Insert the basket into the unit. Select Zone 1 and select AIR FRY. Then set the temperature to 340°F and set the time to 25 minutes. Select START/PAUSE to begin. 3. Drizzle the remaining dressing over the cauliflower and cook at 400°F for about 5 minutes more until the top of the cauliflower is golden brown and the core is tender. 4. Once cooking has finished, remove the basket and transfer the cauliflower to a large plate. Sprinkle with the parsley, if you like, and serve hot.
Per Serving: Calories 142; Fat 11. 57g; Sodium 923mg; Carbs 7g; Fiber 1. 8g; Sugar 2. 21g; Protein 3. 63g

Honey Charred Sweet Potatoes

Prep Time: 15 minutes | Cook Time: 20 minutes | Serves: 2

4 small sweet potatoes, scrubbed clean (3 ounces each)
2 tablespoons olive oil
Kosher salt and freshly ground black pepper

2 tablespoons honey
½ teaspoon smoked paprika
Smoked or regular sea salt, for serving

1. In a bowl, toss together the sweet potatoes with olive oil and season with pepper and kosher salt. Toss again to coat evenly. 2. Install the crisper plate in both baskets, place the sweet potatoes in the baskets, and insert the baskets into the unit. 3. Select Zone 1 and select AIR FRY. Then set the temperature to 375°F and set the time to 20 minutes. Select MATCH COOK to match the Settings in Zone 2 with those in Zone 1. Select START/PAUSE to begin. Flip halfway through until tender on the inside and the skins are crisp and slightly blistered. 4. Meanwhile, in a small bowl, mix together the honey with smoked paprika. 5. When the potatoes are done, split them down the middle like a baked potato and lightly press the ends toward the middle to expose the flesh. Transfer to plates, drizzle with the paprika and honey, and sprinkle with the smoked salt before serving.

Per Serving: Calories 294; Fat 13. 78g; Sodium 1789mg; Carbs 42. 86g; Fiber 4. 4g; Sugar 25. 09g; Protein 2. 62g

Yogurt Caramelized Eggplant

Prep Time: 15 minutes | Cook Time: 15 minutes | Serves: 2

1 medium eggplant (about ¾ pound), cut crosswise into ½-inch-thick slices and quartered
2 tablespoons vegetable oil
Kosher salt and freshly ground black pepper

½ cup plain yogurt (not Greek)
2 tablespoons harissa paste (see Note)
1 garlic clove, grated on a Microplane grater
2 teaspoons honey

1. In a bowl, toss together the eggplant with oil and season with pepper and salt. Toss to coat evenly. 2. Install the crisper plate in the basket, place the eggplant in the basket, and insert the basket into the unit. 3. Select Zone 1 and select AIR FRY. Then set the temperature to 400°F and set the time to 15 minutes. Select START/PAUSE to begin. Shake the basket every 5 minutes until the eggplant is caramelized and tender. 4. Meanwhile, in a small bowl, whisk together the yogurt, harissa, and garlic, then spread onto a serving plate. 5. Once cooking has finished, pile the warm eggplant over the yogurt and drizzle with the honey just before serving.

Per Serving: Calories 256; Fat 16. 14g; Sodium 743mg; Carbs 26. 86g; Fiber 8. 7g; Sugar 19. 04g; Protein 5. 27g

Chili–Roasted Broccoli

Prep Time: 15 minutes | Cook Time: 10 minutes | Serves: 2

12 ounces broccoli florets
2 tablespoons Asian hot chili oil
1 teaspoon ground Sichuan peppercorns (or black pepper)

2 garlic cloves, finely chopped
One 2-inch piece fresh ginger, peeled and finely chopped
Kosher salt and freshly ground black pepper

1. In a bowl, toss together the broccoli, garlic, chili oil, ginger, and salt, Sichuan peppercorns, and black pepper. 2. Install the crisper plate in both baskets, place the broccoli in the baskets, and insert the baskets into the unit. 3. Select Zone 1 and select AIR FRY. Then set the temperature to 375°F and set the time to 10 minutes. Select MATCH COOK to match the Settings in Zone 2 with those in Zone 1. Select START/PAUSE to begin. Shake the basket halfway through until lightly charred and tender. 4. Once cooking has finished, remove and serve warm.

Per Serving: Calories 168; Fat 14. 5g; Sodium 639mg; Carbs 7. 32g; Fiber 5g; Sugar 1. 1g; Protein 5. 84g

Spicy Tahini Kale Leaves

Prep Time: 15 minutes | Cook Time: 15 minutes | Serves: 2-4

¼ cup tahini
¼ cup fresh lemon juice
2 tablespoons olive oil
1 teaspoon sesame seeds
½ teaspoon garlic powder

¼ teaspoon cayenne pepper
4 cups packed torn kale leaves (stems and ribs removed and leaves torn into palm-size pieces; about 4 ounces)
Kosher salt and freshly ground black pepper

1. In a large bowl, whisk together the tahini, garlic powder, olive oil, lemon juice, sesame seeds, and cayenne until smooth. Add the kale leaves and season with salt and black pepper Toss in the dressing until completely coated. 2. Install the crisper plate in the basket, place the kale leaves in the basket, and insert the basket into the unit. 3. Select Zone 1 and select AIR FRY. Then set the temperature to 350°F and set the time to 15 minutes. Select START/PAUSE to begin. Stir every 5 minutes until the kale is wilted and the top is lightly browned. 4. Once cooking has finished, remove and serve warm.

Per Serving: Calories 167; Fat 15. 45g; Sodium 606mg; Carbs 6. 26g; Fiber 2. 2g; Sugar 0. 85g; Protein 3. 54g

Chapter 3 Poultry

Chili Scallion Chicken Patties
Prep Time: 5 minutes | Cook Time: 18 minutes | Serves: 4

⅓ teaspoon paprika
⅓ cup scallions, peeled and chopped
3 cloves garlic, peeled and minced
1 teaspoon ground black pepper, or to taste
½ teaspoon fresh basil, minced

1½ cups chicken, minced
1½ tablespoons coconut aminos
½ teaspoon grated fresh ginger
½ tablespoon chili sauce
1 teaspoon salt

1. Thoroughly combine all ingredients in a mixing dish. Then, form into 4 patties. 2. Install the crisper plate in the basket, place the mixture in the basket, and insert the basket into the unit. 3. Select Zone 1 and select AIR FRY. Then set the temperature to 355°F and set the time to 18 minutes. Select START/PAUSE to begin. 4. Once cooking has finished, garnish with toppings of choice. Bon appétit!
Per Serving: Calories 75; Fat 1. 63g; Sodium 660mg; Carbs 2. 64g; Fiber 0. 7g; Sugar 0. 62g; Protein 12. 05g

Lime and Mustard Chicken
Prep Time: 5 minutes | Cook Time: 26 minutes | Serves: 4

½ teaspoon stone-ground mustard
½ teaspoon minced fresh oregano
⅓ cup freshly squeezed lime juice

2 small-sized chicken breasts, skin-on
1 teaspoon kosher salt
1 teaspoon freshly cracked mixed peppercorns

1. Toss all of the above ingredients in a medium-sized mixing dish and allow it to marinate overnight. 2. Install the crisper plate in the basket, place the mixture in the basket, and insert the basket into the unit. 3. Select Zone 1 and select AIR FRY. Then set the temperature to 345°F and set the time to 26 minutes. Select START/PAUSE to begin. 4. Once cooking has finished, serve. Bon appétit!
Per Serving: Calories 135; Fat 7. 06g; Sodium 628mg; Carbs 1. 93g; Fiber 0. 2g; Sugar 0. 34g; Protein 15. 5g

Spicy Chicken Legs with Brussels Sprouts
Prep Time: 5 minutes | Cook Time: 35 minutes | Serves: 2

2 chicken legs
½ teaspoon paprika
½ teaspoon kosher salt

½ teaspoon black pepper
½ pound Brussels sprouts
1 teaspoon dill, fresh or dried

1. Season the chicken with paprika, pepper and salt. 2. Install the crisper plate in the basket, place the chicken legs in the basket, and insert the basket into the unit. 3. Select Zone 1 and select AIR FRY. Then set the temperature to 370°F and set the time to 10 minutes. Select START/PAUSE to begin. 4. Flip the chicken legs and cook another 10 minutes. Reserve. 5. Add the Brussels sprouts to the cooking basket and sprinkle with dill. Cook at 380°F for 15 minutes and shake the basket halfway through. 6. Once cooking has finished, serve with the reserved chicken legs. Bon appétit!
Per Serving: Calories 370; Fat 11. 63g; Sodium 865mg; Carbs 10. 96g; Fiber 4. 7g; Sugar 2. 56g; Protein 54. 77g

Cheesy Onion Meatballs
Prep Time: 5 minutes | Cook Time: 7 minutes | Serves: 4

1 pound ground turkey
½ pound ground pork
1 egg, well beaten
1 teaspoon dried basil
1 teaspoon dried rosemary

¼ cup Manchego cheese, grated
2 tablespoons yellow onions, finely chopped
1 teaspoon fresh garlic, finely chopped
Sea salt and ground black pepper, to taste

1. Combine all the ingredients in a mixing bowl until everything is well incorporated. Shape the mixture into 1-inch balls. 2. Install the crisper plate in both baskets, place the balls in the baskets, and insert the baskets into the unit. 3. Select Zone 1 and select AIR FRY. Then set the temperature to 380°F and set the time to 7 minutes. Select MATCH COOK to match the Settings in Zone 2 with those in Zone 1. Select START/PAUSE to begin. Shake halfway through the cooking time. 4. Once cooking has finished, serve with your favorite pasta. Bon appétit!
Per Serving: Calories 386; Fat 23. 3g; Sodium 237mg; Carbs 2. 83g; Fiber 0. 4g; Sugar 0. 84g; Protein 40. 39g

Cheesy Butter Chicken Wings
Prep Time: 5 minutes | Cook Time: 22 minutes | Serves: 3

¼ cup almond meal
¼ cup flaxseed meal
2 tablespoons butter, melted
6 tablespoons parmesan cheese, preferably freshly grated

1 tablespoon Ranch seasoning mix
2 tablespoons oyster sauce
6 chicken wings, bone-in

1. In a resealable bag, place the almond meal, butter, parmesan, Ranch seasoning mix, flaxseed meal, and oyster sauce. Add the chicken wings to the bag and shake to coat on all sides. 2. Install the crisper plate in the basket and place the chicken wings in the basket. Insert the basket into the unit. Spritz the chicken wings with a nonstick cooking spray. 3. Select Zone 1 and select AIR FRY. Then set the temperature to 370°F and set the time to 11 minutes. Select START/PAUSE to begin. 4. Turn them over and cook another 11 minutes. 5. Once cooking has finished, serve warm with your favorite dipping sauce, if desired. Enjoy!
Per Serving: Calories 274; Fat 18. 5g; Sodium 827mg; Carbs 8. 43g; Fiber 4. 3g; Sugar 0. 54g; Protein 18. 54g

Lemony Turkey Breasts with Basil
Prep Time: 5 minutes | Cook Time: 58 minutes | Serves: 4

2 tablespoons olive oil
2 pounds turkey breasts, bone-in skin-on
Coarse sea salt and ground black pepper, to taste

1 teaspoon fresh basil leaves, chopped
2 tablespoons lemon zest, grated

1. Rub olive oil on all sides of the turkey breasts and sprinkle with salt, basil, pepper, and lemon zest. 2. Install the crisper plate in both baskets, place the turkey breasts skin side up on parchment-lined baskets, and insert the baskets into the unit. 3. Select Zone 1 and select AIR FRY. Then set the temperature to 330°F and set the time to 30 minutes. Select MATCH COOK to match the Settings in Zone 2 with those in Zone 1. Select START/PAUSE to begin. 4. Now, turn them over and cook another 28 minutes. 5. Once cooking has finished, serve with lemon wedges, if desired. Bon appétit!
Per Serving: Calories 495; Fat 23. 6g; Sodium 144mg; Carbs 1. 59g; Fiber 0. 2g; Sugar 0. 77g; Protein 65. 37g

Garlicy Turkey Wings

Prep Time: 5 minutes | Cook Time: 28 minutes | Serves: 4

1 teaspoon freshly cracked pink peppercorns
1½ pound turkey wings, cut into smaller pieces
2 teaspoon garlic powder

⅓ cup white wine
½ teaspoon garlic salt
½ tablespoon coriander, ground

1. Toss all of the above ingredients in a mixing dish. Let it marinate at least 3 hours. 2. Install the crisper plate in the basket, place the turkey wings in the basket, and insert the basket into the unit. 3. Select Zone 1 and select AIR FRY. Then set the temperature to 355°F and set the time to 28 minutes. Select START/ PAUSE to begin. 4. Once cooking has finished, serve. Bon appétit!
Per Serving: Calories 346; Fat 20. 99g; Sodium 96mg; Carbs 2. 09g; Fiber 0. 3g; Sugar 0. 25g; Protein 35. 01g

Hoisin Butted Turkey Drumstick

Prep Time: 5 minutes | Cook Time: 40 minutes | Serves: 4

2 pounds turkey drumsticks
2 tablespoons balsamic vinegar
2 tablespoons dry white wine
1 tablespoon sesame oil
For the Hoisin Sauce:
2 tablespoons hoisin sauce

1 sprig rosemary, chopped
Salt and ground black pepper, to your liking
2 ½ tablespoons butter, melted

1 tablespoon mustard

1. Add the turkey drumsticks to a mixing dish and add the vinegar, sesame oil, wine, and rosemary. Let them marinate for 3 hours. 2. Season the turkey drumsticks with salt and black pepper and spread the melted butter over the surface of drumsticks. 3. Install the crisper plate in both baskets, place the turkey drumsticks in the baskets, and insert the baskets into the unit. 4. Select Zone 1 and select AIR FRY. Then set the temperature to 350°F and set the time to 35 minutes. Select MATCH COOK to match the Settings in Zone 2 with those in Zone 1. Select START/PAUSE to begin. 5. Turn the drumsticks over a few times during the cooking. 6. While the turkey drumsticks are roasting, prepare the Hoisin sauce by mixing the ingredients. 7. After that, drizzle the turkey with the sauce mixture and roast for a further 5 minutes. 8. Once cooking has finished, allow it to rest about 10 minutes before carving and serving. Bon appétit!
Per Serving: Calories 541; Fat 24. 25g; Sodium 383mg; Carbs 11. 56g; Fiber 1. 1g; Sugar 4. 01g; Protein 65. 39g

Almond Chicken Breasts with Scallion

Prep Time: 5 minutes | Cook Time: 30 minutes | Serves: 4

2 chicken breasts, cut into bite-sized chunks
⅓ cup almond flour
1 cup scallions, chopped
1 celery, chopped

For the Sauce:
¼ cup dry white wine
2 tablespoons coconut aminos
½ cup of chicken broth

1. Toss the chicken chunks with the almond flour and cover well. 2. Install the crisper plate in the basket, place the chicken chunks in the basket, and insert the basket into the unit. 3. Select Zone 1 and select AIR FRY. Then set the temperature to 365°F and set the time to 20 minutes. Select START/PAUSE to begin. 4. Pause to add the vegetables into the cooking basket and cook for a further 5 to 7 minutes. 5. Meanwhile, in a sauté pan, whisk the remaining ingredients over a moderate flame and turn the temperature to medium-low and cook for 2 to 3 minutes. 6. Once cooking has finished, serve the chicken with the warm sauce and enjoy!
Per Serving: Calories 331; Fat 17. 12g; Sodium 357mg; Carbs 3. 24g; Fiber 1. 1g; Sugar 1. 15g; Protein 38. 91g

Juicy Chicken Nuggets

Prep Time: 10 minutes | Cook Time: 60 minutes | Serves: 4

4 (8-ounce) boneless, skinless chicken breasts, trimmed
Salt and pepper
3 tablespoons sugar
3 cups panko bread crumbs
¼ cup extra-virgin olive oil

3 large eggs
3 tablespoons all-purpose flour
1 tablespoon onion powder
¾ teaspoon garlic powder

1. Pound the chicken to uniform thickness as needed. Cut each breast diagonally into thirds, then cut each piece into thirds. Dissolve 3 tablespoons salt and sugar in 2-quart cold water in a large container. Place in the chicken, cover, and allow to sit for 15 minutes. 2. Meanwhile, toss the panko with oil in a bowl until evenly coated. Microwave for about 5 minutes, stirring frequently, until light golden brown. Transfer to a shallow dish and allow to cool slightly. Whisk the eggs, flour, garlic powder, onion powder, 1 teaspoon salt, and ¼ teaspoon pepper together in the second shallow dish. 3. Set the wire rack in rimmed baking sheet. Take the chicken out of brine and pat dry with paper towels. Working with several chicken pieces at a time, dredge in egg mixture, letting excess drip off, and then coat with panko mixture, pressing gently to adhere. Transfer to the prepared rack. Freeze until firm, about 4 hours. 4. Lightly spray base of crisper plates with vegetable oil spray. Install the crisper plate in both baskets, put the nuggets in the baskets, and insert the baskets into the unit. 5. Select Zone 1 and select AIR FRY. Then set the temperature to 400°F and set the time to 6 minutes. Select MATCH COOK to match the Settings in Zone 2 with those in Zone 1. Then select START/PAUSE to begin. 6. Transfer the nuggets to a clean bowl and gently toss to redistribute. Return nuggets to the basket and cook until chicken is crisp and registers 160°F, 6 to 10 minutes. 7. Once cooking has finished, serve. You can serve with the sweet-and-sour dipping sauce. To make the sauce: Whisk ¾ cup apple jelly, 1 tablespoon distilled white vinegar, ½ teaspoon soy sauce, ⅛ teaspoon garlic powder, pinch ground ginger, and pinch cayenne pepper together in bowl; season with salt and pepper to taste. Sauce can be refrigerated for up to 4 days and bring to room temperature before serving. You can also serve with the honey-dijon dipping sauce. To make this sauce: Whisk ½ cup Dijon mustard and ¼ cup honey together in bowl; season with salt and pepper to taste. Store in the refrigerator for up to 4 days and bring to room temperature before serving.
Per Serving: Calories 500; Fat 13. 74g; Sodium 1755mg; Carbs 72. 27g; Fiber 4. 3g; Sugar 11. 15g; Protein 20. 88g

Lime Nut–Crusted Chicken Breasts

Prep Time: 10 minutes | Cook Time: 12 minutes | Serves: 2

½ cup slivered almonds, chopped fine
½ cup panko bread crumbs
2 tablespoons unsalted butter, melted
1 teaspoon grated lemon zest, plus lemon wedges for serving
Salt and pepper

1 large egg
1 tablespoon all-purpose flour
1 teaspoon minced fresh thyme or ½ teaspoon dried
Pinch cayenne pepper
2 (8-ounce) boneless, skinless chicken breasts, trimmed

1. Combine the panko, almonds, lemon zest, melted butter, and ¼ teaspoon salt in a bowl and microwave for about 4 minutes, stirring occasionally, until panko is light golden brown and almonds are fragrant. Transfer to a shallow dish and set aside to cool slightly. Whisk the thyme, egg, flour, and cayenne together in the second shallow dish. 2. Pound the chicken to uniform thickness as needed. Pat dry with the paper towels and season with the salt and pepper. Working with one breast at a time, suck in the egg mixture and let the excess drip off, and then coat with the panko mixture, pressing gently to stick. 3. Lightly spray base of crisper plates with vegetable oil spray. Install the crisper plate in both baskets, put the breasts in the baskets, spaced evenly apart, alternating ends. Insert the baskets into the unit. 4. Select Zone 1 and select AIR FRY. Then set the temperature to 400°F and set the time to 16 minutes. Select MATCH COOK to match the Settings in Zone 2 with those in Zone 1. Then select START/PAUSE to begin. Cook for 12 to 16 minutes until chicken is crisp and registers 160°F, flipping and rotating the breasts halfway through cooking. 5. Once cooking has finished, serve with the lemon wedges.
Per Serving: Calories 247; Fat 12. 42g; Sodium 2208mg; Carbs 14. 61g; Fiber 1g; Sugar 3. 09g; Protein 20. 37g

Spicy Chicken–Lettuce Sandwich

Prep Time: 10 minutes | Cook Time: 12 minutes | Serves: 4

1 cup panko bread crumbs
2 tablespoons extra-virgin olive oil
1 large egg
3 tablespoons hot sauce
1 tablespoon all-purpose flour
½ teaspoon garlic powder

Salt and pepper
2 (8-ounce) boneless, skinless chicken breasts, trimmed
¼ cup mayonnaise
4 hamburger buns, toasted if desired
2 cups shredded iceberg lettuce
¼ cup jarred sliced jalapeños

1 Toss the panko with the oil in a bowl until evenly coated. Microwave for 1 to 3 minutes, stirring frequently, until light golden brown. Transfer to a shallow dish and set aside to cool slightly. Whisk the flour, egg, 2 tablespoons hot sauce, garlic powder, ⅛ teaspoon salt, and ⅛ teaspoon pepper together in the second shallow dish. 2. Pound the chicken to uniform thickness as needed. Halve each breast crosswise, pat dry with the paper towels, and season with the pepper and salt. Working with 1 piece of chicken at a time, dredge in the egg mixture, letting excess drip off, and then coat with the panko mixture, pressing gently to adhere. 3. Lightly spray base of crisper plate with vegetable oil spray. Install the crisper plate in both baskets, put the chicken pieces in the baskets, spacing evenly apart and insert the baskets into the unit. 4. Select Zone 1 and select AIR FRY. Then set the temperature to 400°F and set the time to 16 minutes. Select MATCH COOK to match the Settings in Zone 2 with those in Zone 1. Then select START/PAUSE to begin. Cook for 12 to 16 minutes until chicken is crisp and registers 160°F, flipping and rotating chicken pieces halfway through cooking. 5. Combine the mayonnaise and remaining 1 tablespoon hot sauce in a small bowl. 6. Once cooking has finished, spread mayonnaise mixture evenly over bun bottoms, then top with 1 piece chicken, lettuce, jalapeños, and bun tops. Serve.

Per Serving: Calories 360; Fat 16. 72g; Sodium 1290mg; Carbs 30. 33g; Fiber 2. 2g; Sugar 4. 79g; Protein 21. 4g

Homemade Chicken Parmesan

Prep Time: 10 minutes | Cook Time: 13 minutes | Serves: 2

¾ cup panko bread crumbs
2 tablespoons extra-virgin olive oil
¼ cup grated Parmesan cheese
1 large egg
1 tablespoon all-purpose flour
¾ teaspoon garlic powder

½ teaspoon dried oregano
Salt and pepper
2 (8-ounce) boneless, skinless chicken breasts, trimmed
2 ounces whole-milk mozzarella cheese, shredded (½ cup)
¼ cup jarred marinara sauce, warmed
2 tablespoons chopped fresh basil

1. Toss the panko with the oil in a bowl until evenly coated. Microwave for 1 to 3 minutes and stir frequently until light golden brown. 2. Transfer to a shallow dish, let cool slightly, then stir in Parmesan. 3. Whisk the egg, garlic powder, flour, ⅛ teaspoon salt, oregano, and ⅛ teaspoon pepper together in the second shallow dish. 4. Pound the chicken to uniform thickness as needed. Pat dry with the paper towels and season with the pepper and salt. Working with 1 breast at a time, dredge in the egg mixture, letting excess drip off, then coat with the panko mixture, pressing gently to adhere. 5. Lightly spray base of crisper plates with vegetable oil spray. Install the crisper plate in both baskets, put the breasts in the baskets, spaced evenly apart, alternating ends. Insert the baskets into the unit. 6. Select Zone 1 and select AIR FRY. Then set the temperature to 400°F and set the time to 16 minutes. Select MATCH COOK to match the Settings in Zone 2 with those in Zone 1. Then select START/PAUSE to begin. Cook for 12 to 16 minutes until chicken is crisp and registers 160°F, flipping and rotating breasts halfway through cooking. 7. Sprinkle the chicken with mozzarella and cook for about 1 minute until cheese is melted. 8. Once cooking has finished, transfer the chicken to individual serving plates. Top each breast with 2 tablespoons warm marinara sauce and sprinkle with basil. Serve.

Per Serving: Calories 330; Fat 21. 03g; Sodium 1832mg; Carbs 19. 18g; Fiber 1. 6g; Sugar 2. 93g; Protein 16. 13g

Cheesy–Mayo Ham Chicken Breasts

Prep Time: 10 minutes | Cook Time: 13 minutes | Serves: 2

2 (8-ounce) boneless, skinless chicken breasts, trimmed
Salt and pepper
4 thick slices ham (4 ounces)
2 slices Swiss cheese (2 ounces)

2 tablespoons mayonnaise
1 tablespoon Dijon mustard
1 teaspoon water
1 tablespoon minced fresh chives

1. Pound the chicken to uniform thickness as needed. Pat dry with the paper towels and season with salt and pepper. For each chicken breast, shingle 2 slices of ham on counter, overlapping edges slightly, and lay the chicken, skinned side down, in center. Fold the ham around chicken and secure overlapping ends by threading toothpick through the ham and chicken. Flip the chicken and thread toothpick through ham and chicken on second side. 2. Lightly spray base of crisper plates with vegetable oil spray. Install the crisper plate in both baskets. Arrange breasts skinned side down in the basket, spaced evenly apart, alternating ends. Insert the baskets into the unit. Select Zone 1 and select AIR FRY. Then set the temperature to 400°F and set the time to 16 minutes. Select MATCH COOK to match the Settings in Zone 2 with those in Zone 1. Then select START/PAUSE to begin. Cook until edges of ham begin to brown and chicken registers 160°F, 12 to 16 minutes. Flip and rotate the breasts halfway through cooking. Top each breast with 1 slice Swiss, folding cheese as needed. Return the basket to air fryer and cook until cheese is melted, about 1 minute. 3. When cooking is up, transfer the chicken to a serving platter and discard toothpicks. Tent loosely with the aluminum foil and let rest for 5 minutes. Meanwhile, combine the mustard, mayonnaise, and water in a small bowl. Drizzle chicken with 1 tablespoon sauce and sprinkle with chives. Serve, passing remaining sauce separately.
Per Serving: Calories 411; Fat 24. 92g; Sodium 2046mg; Carbs 5. 06g; Fiber 0. 9g; Sugar 1. 74g; Protein 40. 64g

Spicy Chicken Breasts with Vegetable Salad

Prep Time: 10 minutes | Cook Time: 20 minutes | Serves: 2

1 cup canned cannellini beans, rinsed
2 tablespoons extra-virgin olive oil
1½ tablespoons red wine vinegar
1 garlic clove, minced
Salt and pepper
½ red onion, sliced thin

8 ounces asparagus, trimmed and cut into 1-inch lengths
½ teaspoon ground coriander
¼ teaspoon paprika
2 (8-ounce) boneless, skinless chicken breasts, trimmed
2 ounces (2 cups) baby arugula

1. Microwave the beans in a large bowl until just warm, about 30 seconds. Stir in 1 tablespoon oil, garlic, ¼ teaspoon salt, vinegar, and pinch pepper and set aside. 2. Toss the onion with 2 teaspoons oil, ⅛ teaspoon salt, and pinch pepper in a clean bowl to coat. Install the crisper plate in the basket, put the onion in the basket, and insert the basket into the unit. Select Zone 1 and select AIR FRY. Then set the temperature to 400°F and set the time to 2 minutes. Select START/PAUSE to begin. After cooking for 2 minutes, stir in asparagus, return the basket to air fryer, and cook for 6 to 8 minutes until asparagus is tender and bright green, tossing halfway through cooking. 3. When cooking is up, transfer to a bowl with beans and set aside. 4. Combine the coriander, ¼ teaspoon salt, paprika, and ⅛ teaspoon pepper in a small bowl. Pound the chicken to uniform thickness as needed. Pat dry with the paper towels, rub with remaining 1 teaspoon oil, and sprinkle evenly with spice mixture. Install the crisper plate in both baskets. Arrange breasts skinned side down in the baskets, spaced evenly apart, alternating ends. Insert the baskets into the unit. Select Zone 1 and select AIR FRY. Then set the temperature to 400°F and set the time to 16 minutes. Select MATCH COOK to match the Settings in Zone 2 with those in Zone 1. Then select START/PAUSE to begin. Cook for 12 to 16 minutes until the chicken registers 160°F, flipping and rotating breasts halfway through cooking. 5. Once cooking has finished, transfer the chicken to a serving platter, tent loosely with the aluminum foil, and let rest for 5 minutes. Add the arugula to asparagus mixture in a bowl and toss to combine. Season with salt and pepper to taste. Serve chicken with salad.
Per Serving: Calories 311; Fat 17. 26g; Sodium 1369mg; Carbs 11. 77g; Fiber 4. 8g; Sugar 4. 6g; Protein 28. 4g

Thyme Apricot–Glazed Chicken Breasts
Prep Time: 10 minutes | Cook Time: 12 minutes | Serves: 2

2 tablespoons apricot preserves
½ teaspoon minced fresh thyme or ⅛ teaspoon dried
2 (8-ounce) boneless, skinless chicken breasts, trimmed

1 teaspoon vegetable oil
Salt and pepper

1. Microwave the apricot preserves and thyme in a bowl for about 30 seconds until fluid and set aside. Pound the chicken to uniform thickness as needed. Pat dry with paper towels, rub with oil, and season with salt and pepper. 2. Install the crisper plate in both baskets. Arrange breasts skinned side down in the baskets spaced evenly apart, alternating ends. Insert the baskets into the unit. 3. Select Zone 1 and select AIR FRY. Then set the temperature to 400°F and set the time to 4 minutes. Select MATCH COOK to match the Settings in Zone 2 with those in Zone 1. Then select START/PAUSE to begin. 4. Flip and rotate chicken, then brush skinned side with apricot-thyme mixture. Return the basket to air fryer and cook for 8 to 12 minutes until chicken registers 160°F. 5. When cooking is up, transfer the chicken to a serving platter. Tent the chicken loosely with aluminum foil and let rest for 5 minutes. Serve.

Per Serving: Calories 111; Fat 4. 95g; Sodium 1184mg; Carbs 10. 77g; Fiber 1g; Sugar 9. 1g; Protein 6. 58g

Super–Easy Chicken Breasts
Prep Time: 10 minutes | Cook Time: 20 minutes | Serves: 2

2 (12-ounce) bone-in split chicken breasts, trimmed
1 teaspoon extra-virgin olive oil

Salt and pepper

1. Pat the chicken dry with paper towels, rub with oil, and season with salt and pepper. 2. Install the crisper plate in the basket. Arrange breasts skin side down in the basket spaced evenly apart, alternating ends. Insert the basket into the unit. 3. Select Zone 1 and select AIR FRY. Then set the temperature to 350°F and set the time to 25 minutes. Select START/PAUSE to begin. Cook for 20 to 25 minutes until chicken registers 160°F, flipping and rotating breasts halfway through cooking. 4. Once cooking has finished, transfer the chicken to a serving platter, tent loosely with the aluminum foil, and let rest for 5 minutes. Serve.

Per Serving: Calories 310; Fat 16. 74g; Sodium 1291mg; Carbs 2. 13g; Fiber 0. 3g; Sugar 1. 15g; Protein 35. 92g

Garlic Sausages with Ground Chicken
Prep Time: 20 minutes | Cook Time: 23 minutes | Serves: 4

1 garlic clove, diced
1 spring onion, chopped
1 cup ground chicken
½ teaspoon salt

½ teaspoon ground black pepper
4 sausage links
1 teaspoon olive oil

1. In the mixing bowl, mix up a diced garlic clove, ground chicken, salt, onion, and ground black pepper. 2. Then fill the sausage links with the ground chicken mixture. Cut every sausage into halves and secure the endings. 3. Brush the sausages with olive oil. Install the crisper plate in both baskets, put the sausages in the baskets, and insert the baskets into the unit. 4. Select Zone 1 and select AIR FRY. Then set the temperature to 365°F and set the time to 10 minutes. Select MATCH COOK to match the Settings in Zone 2 with those in Zone 1. Then select START/PAUSE to begin. 5. After cooking for 10 minutes, flip the sausages on another side and cook for 5 minutes more. Increase the cooking temperature to 390°F and cook for 8 minutes for faster results. 6. Once cooking has finished, serve.

Per Serving: Calories 113; Fat 6. 86g; Sodium 537mg; Carbs 3. 52g; Fiber 0. 9g; Sugar 0. 38g; Protein 10. 33g

Cream Chicken Turkey with Cherry Tomatoes

Prep Time: 5 minutes | Cook Time: 25 minutes | Serves: 4

1 pound turkey breast, skinless, boneless and cubed
1 cup heavy cream
A pinch of salt and black pepper
4 ounces cherry tomatoes, halved

1 tablespoon ginger, grated
2 tablespoons red chili powder
2 teaspoons olive oil

1. Heat up a saucepan with the oil over medium heat. Add the turkey and brown for 2 minutes on each side. Place in the rest of the ingredients and toss. 2. Install the crisper plate in the basket, put the mixture in the basket, and insert the basket into the unit. Select Zone 1 and select AIR FRY. Then set the temperature to 380°F and set the time to 20 minutes. Select START/PAUSE to begin. 3. Once cooking has finished, divide everything between plates and serve.

Per Serving: Calories 336; Fat 21. 97g; Sodium 194mg; Carbs 8. 69g; Fiber 2. 2g; Sugar 5. 36g; Protein 26. 53g

Coconut Turmeric Chicken Strips

Prep Time: 15 minutes | Cook Time: 7 minutes | Serves: 6

2-pound chicken breast, skinless, boneless
1 teaspoon salt
1 teaspoon ground turmeric

½ teaspoon cayenne pepper
1 egg, beaten
2 tablespoons coconut flour

1. Cut the chicken breast into the strips and sprinkle with salt, ground turmeric, and cayenne pepper. 2. Then add beaten egg in the chicken strips and stir the mixture. After this, add coconut flour and stir it. 3. Install the crisper plate in both baskets, put all chicken strips in the baskets in one layer, and insert the baskets into the unit. Select Zone 1 and select AIR FRY. Then set the temperature to 400°F and set the time to 7 minutes. Select MATCH COOK to match the Settings in Zone 2 with those in Zone 1. Then select START/PAUSE to begin. 4. Once cooking has finished, serve.

Per Serving: Calories 242; Fat 7. 06g; Sodium 906mg; Carbs 0. 78g; Fiber 0. 2g; Sugar 0. 27g; Protein 43. 99g

Tasty Chicken Paillard

Prep Time: 20 minutes | Cook Time: 10 minutes | Serves: 4

1 pound boneless, skinless chicken breasts or thighs
2 tablespoons avocado oil
1 tablespoon freshly squeezed lemon juice
1 teaspoon chopped fresh oregano

½ teaspoon garlic powder
Sea salt
Freshly ground black pepper

1. Place the chicken in a zip-top bag or between two pieces of plastic wrap. Pound the chicken with a meat mallet or a heavy skillet until it is very thin, about ¼ inch thick. 2. In a small bowl, combine the avocado oil, garlic powder, oregano, salt, lemon juice, and pepper. Place the chicken in a shallow dish and pour the marinade over it. Toss to coat all the chicken, and allow to rest at room temperature for 10 to 15 minutes. 3. Install the crisper plate in the basket, place the chicken in a single layer in the basket. Insert the basket into the unit. Select Zone 1 and select AIR FRY. Then set the temperature to 400°F and set the time to 5 minutes. Select START/PAUSE to begin. Flip and cook for another 2 to 5 minutes, until an instant-read thermometer reads 160°F. 4. Once cooking has finished, allow to rest for 5 minutes before serving.

Per Serving: Calories 236; Fat 11. 02g; Sodium 801mg; Carbs 0. 92g; Fiber 0. 2g; Sugar 0. 12g; Protein 32. 07g

Cheesy Chicken Pockets

Prep Time: 15 minutes | Cook Time: 4 minutes | Serves: 4

2 low carb tortillas
2 oz Cheddar cheese, grated
1 tomato, chopped
1 teaspoon fresh cilantro, chopped
½ teaspoon dried basil

2 teaspoons butter
6 oz chicken fillet, boiled
1 teaspoon sunflower oil
½ teaspoon salt

1. Cut the tortillas into halves. Shred the chicken fillet with the fork and put it in the bowl. Add grated cheese, chopped tomato, cilantro, basil, and salt. 2. Then grease the tortilla halves with butter from one side. Put the shredded chicken mixture on half of every tortilla piece and fold them into the pockets. 3. Brush every tortilla pocket with sunflower oil. Install the crisper plate in both baskets, put the tortilla pockets in the baskets, and insert the baskets into the unit. Select Zone 1 and select AIR FRY. Then set the temperature to 400°F and set the time to 4 minutes. Select MATCH COOK to match the Settings in Zone 2 with those in Zone 1. Then select START/PAUSE to begin. 4. Once cooking has finished, serve.

Per Serving: Calories 187; Fat 9. 2g; Sodium 656mg; Carbs 14. 81g; Fiber 1g; Sugar 2. 6g; Protein 11. 5g

Chili Chicken Wonton Rolls

Prep Time: 10 minutes | Cook Time: 15 minutes | Serves: 4

4 wonton wraps
8 oz chicken fillet
1 garlic clove, diced
1 teaspoon keto tomato sauce

1 teaspoon butter, melted
¼ teaspoon chili flakes
½ teaspoon ground turmeric

1. Slice the chicken on the small strips and sprinkle with ground turmeric, chili flakes, and butter. 2. Install the crisper plate in both baskets, put the sliced chicken in the baskets, and insert the baskets into the unit. Select Zone 1 and select AIR FRY. Then set the temperature to 365°F and set the time to 10 minutes. Select MATCH COOK to match the Settings in Zone 2 with those in Zone 1. Then select START/PAUSE to begin. 3. Once cooking has finished, then transfer the chicken in the bowl. Add tomato sauce and diced garlic. Mix up the chicken and place it on the wonton wraps. Roll them. Serve.

Per Serving: Calories 117; Fat 5. 71g; Sodium 112mg; Carbs 5. 52g; Fiber 0. 4g; Sugar 0. 18g; Protein 10. 83g

Buttermilk–Fried Chicken Drumsticks

Prep Time: 10 minutes | Cook Time: 25 minutes | Serves: 4

1 egg
½ cup buttermilk
¾ cup self-rising flour
¾ cup seasoned panko breadcrumbs

1 teaspoon salt
¼ teaspoon ground black pepper (to mix into coating)
4 chicken drumsticks, skin on
Oil for misting or cooking spray

1. Beat together egg and buttermilk in shallow dish. 2. In a second shallow dish, combine the salt, flour, panko crumbs, and pepper. 3. Sprinkle chicken legs with additional salt and pepper. 4. Dip legs in buttermilk mixture and then roll in panko mixture, pressing in crumbs to make coating stick. Mist with oil or cooking spray. 5. Spray the crisper plate with cooking spray. 6. Install the crisper plate in both baskets, place the drumsticks in the baskets, and insert the baskets into the unit. Select Zone 1 and select AIR FRY. Then set the temperature to 360°F and set the time to 10 minutes. Select START/PAUSE to begin. Turn pieces over and cook another 10 minutes. 7. Turn pieces to check for browning. If you have any white spots that haven't begun to brown, spritz them with oil or cooking spray. Continue cooking for 5 more minutes or until crust is golden brown and juices run clear. Larger, meatier drumsticks will take longer to cook than small ones. 8. Once cooking has finished, serve.

Per Serving: Calories 421; Fat 14. 93g; Sodium 2930mg; Carbs 34. 43g; Fiber 4. 1g; Sugar 4. 6g; Protein 30. 29g

Coconut Chicken Wings

Prep Time: 15 minutes | Cook Time: 20 minutes | Serves: 6

6 chicken wings
1 tablespoon coconut aminos
1 teaspoon ground ginger
1 teaspoon salt

1 teaspoon minced garlic
2 tablespoons apple cider vinegar
1 tablespoon olive oil
1 chili pepper, chopped

1. Put the chicken wings in the bowl and sprinkle with coconut aminos and ground ginger. Add salt, apple cider vinegar, minced garlic, olive oil, and chopped chili. 2. Mix up the chicken wings and leave them for 15 minutes to marinate. 3. Install the crisper plate in both baskets, put the marinated chicken wings in the baskets, and insert the baskets into the unit. Select Zone 1 and select AIR FRY. Then set the temperature to 380°F and set the time to 20 minutes. Select MATCH COOK to match the Settings in Zone 2 with those in Zone 1. Then select START/PAUSE to begin. 4. Flip the chicken wings from time to time to avoid the burning. 5. Once cooking has finished, serve.

Per Serving: Calories 63; Fat 3. 31g; Sodium 415mg; Carbs 1. 22g; Fiber 0. 2g; Sugar 0. 48g; Protein 6. 6g

Tender Coconut Chicken

Prep Time: 5 minutes | Cook Time: 15 minutes | Serves: 4

¾ cup of buttermilk
1½ pounds chicken tenders
½ cup coconut flour
2 tablespoons flaxseed meal
Salt, to your liking

½ teaspoon pink peppercorns, freshly cracked
1 teaspoon shallot powder
½ teaspoon cumin powder
1½ teaspoon smoked cayenne pepper
1 tablespoon sesame oil

1. Place the buttermilk and chicken tenders in the mixing dish, gently stir to coat, and let it soak for 1 hour. 2. Then, mix the coconut flour with flaxseed meal and all seasonings. Coat the soaked chicken tenders with the coconut flour mixture. Dip them into the buttermilk. Dredge them in the coconut flour mixture. 3. Brush the prepared chicken tenders with sesame oil. Install the crisper plate in the basket, place the chicken tenders in the basket, and insert the basket into the unit. 4. Select Zone 1 and select AIR FRY. Then set the temperature to 365°F and set the time to 15 minutes. Select START/PAUSE to begin. Make sure to shake them once or twice. 5. Once cooking has finished, serve. Bon appétit!

Per Serving: Calories 516; Fat 28. 15g; Sodium 1461mg; Carbs 35. 55g; Fiber 2g; Sugar 3. 17g; Protein 30. 75g

Spicy Butter Turkey Breast

Prep Time: 5 minutes | Cook Time: 55 minutes | Serves: 10

1 tablespoon sea salt
1 teaspoon paprika
1 teaspoon onion powder
1 teaspoon garlic powder

½ teaspoon freshly ground black pepper
4 pounds bone-in, skin-on turkey breast
2 tablespoons unsalted butter, melted

1. Combine the salt, onion powder, paprika, garlic powder, and pepper in a small bowl. 2. Sprinkle the seasonings all over the turkey. Brush the turkey with the melted butter. 3. Install the crisper plate in both baskets, place the turkey, skin-side down, in the baskets, and insert the baskets into the unit. Select Zone 1 and select AIR FRY. Then set the temperature to 350°F and set the time to 25 minutes. Select MATCH COOK to match the Settings in Zone 2 with those in Zone 1. Select START/PAUSE to begin. 4. Flip the turkey and brush it with the remaining butter. Cook for another 20 to 30 minutes until an instant-read thermometer reads 160°F. 5. Once cooking has finished, remove the turkey breast. Tent a piece of aluminum foil over the turkey, and allow it to rest for about 5 minutes before serving.

Per Serving: Calories 247; Fat 7. 88g; Sodium 1420mg; Carbs 1. 05g; Fiber 0. 3g; Sugar 0. 05g; Protein 40. 49g

Crispy Buffalo Chicken Tenders

Prep Time: 15 minutes | Cook Time: 10 minutes | Serves: 4

½ cup finely ground blanched almond flour
½ cup finely grated Parmesan cheese
1 teaspoon smoked paprika
¼ teaspoon cayenne pepper
½ teaspoon sea salt, plus additional for seasoning, divided
Freshly ground black pepper
2 large eggs
1 pound chicken tenders

Avocado oil spray
⅓ cup hot sauce, such as Frank's RedHot
2 tablespoons unsalted butter
2 tablespoons white vinegar
1 garlic clove, minced
Blue Cheese Dressing, for serving
Blue cheese crumbles, for serving

1. In a shallow bowl, combine the almond flour, smoked paprika, Parmesan cheese, and cayenne pepper and season with salt and pepper. Beat the eggs in a separate shallow bowl. 2. One at a time, dip the chicken tenders in the eggs and then coat them with the almond flour mixture, pressing the coating into the chicken gently. 3. Install the crisper plate in the basket, place the chicken tenders in a single layer in the basket and spray them with oil. Insert the basket into the unit. 4. Select Zone 1 and select AIR FRY. Then set the temperature to 400°F and set the time to 4 minutes. Select START/PAUSE to begin. Flip the tenders and spray them with more oil. Cook for 3 to 6 minutes more or until an instant-read thermometer reads 165°F. 5. While cooking the chicken, add the hot sauce, vinegar, garlic, butter, and ½ teaspoon of salt in a small saucepan over medium-low heat. Cook until the butter is melted and whisk to combine. 6. Once cooking has finished, toss the chicken tenders with the sauce. Serve warm with Blue Cheese Dressing and blue cheese crumbles.

Per Serving: Calories 475; Fat 30. 55g; Sodium 1419mg; Carbs 9. 49g; Fiber 2. 2g; Sugar 1. 57g; Protein 40. 57g

Classic Nashville Hot Chicken

Prep Time: 5 minutes | Cook Time: 28 minutes | Serves: 8

3 pounds bone-in, skin-on chicken pieces, breasts halved crosswise
1 tablespoon sea salt
1 tablespoon freshly ground black pepper
1½ cups finely ground blanched almond flour
1½ cups grated Parmesan cheese
1 tablespoon baking powder
2 teaspoons garlic powder, divided

½ cup heavy (whipping) cream
2 large eggs, beaten
1 tablespoon vinegar-based hot sauce
Avocado oil spray
½ cup (1 stick) unsalted butter
½ cup avocado oil
1 tablespoon cayenne pepper (more or less to taste)
2 tablespoons brown sugar substitute, such as Sukrin Gold

1. Sprinkle the chicken with the pepper and salt. 2. In a large shallow bowl, whisk together the baking powder, almond flour, Parmesan cheese, and 1 teaspoon of the garlic powder. 3. Whisk together the eggs, heavy cream, and hot sauce in a separate bowl. 4. Dip the chicken in the egg and then coat each with the almond flour mixture, ensuring to press the mixture into the chicken to adhere. Allow to sit for 15 minutes to let the breading set. 5. Install the crisper plate in both baskets, place the chicken in a single layer in the baskets, spraying chicken with oil, and insert the baskets into the unit. Select Zone 1 and select AIR FRY. Then set the temperature to 400°F and set the time to 13 minutes. Select MATCH COOK to match the Settings in Zone 2 with those in Zone 1. Select START/PAUSE to begin. 6. Carefully flip the chicken and spray it with more oil. Reduce the heat to 350°F. Cook for another 11 to 15 minutes until an instant-read thermometer reads 160°F. 7. While the chicken cooks, heat the butter, cayenne pepper, brown sugar substitute, avocado oil, and remaining 1 teaspoon of garlic powder in a saucepan over medium-low heat. Cook until the butter is melted and the sugar substitute has dissolved. 8. Once cooking has finished, remove the chicken. Dip the chicken in the sauce with tongs. Place the coated chicken on a rack over a baking sheet to let it rest for 5 minutes before serving.

Per Serving: Calories 627; Fat 46. 76g; Sodium 1378mg; Carbs 8. 34g; Fiber 0. 6g; Sugar 1. 1g; Protein 42. 7g

Barbecue Ketchup Turkey Meatballs

Prep Time: 20 minutes | Cook Time: 2 minutes | Serves: 4

1 pound ground turkey
½ teaspoon sea salt, plus additional to season the ground turkey
Freshly ground black pepper
1 large egg, beaten
1 teaspoon gelatin
½ cup almond meal
½ tablespoon chili powder
2½ teaspoons smoked paprika, divided
1 teaspoon onion powder
2 teaspoons garlic powder, divided
Avocado oil spray
¾ cup sugar-free ketchup
1 tablespoon yellow mustard
1 tablespoon apple cider vinegar
2 tablespoons brown sugar substitute, such as Swerve or Sukrin Gold
1 teaspoon liquid smoke

1. Place the ground turkey in a large bowl and season with pepper and salt. 2. Place the beaten egg in a bowl and sprinkle with the gelatin. Allow to rest for 5 minutes and whisk to combine. 3. Pour the gelatin mixture over the ground turkey and add the almond meal, 1 teaspoon of smoked paprika, chili powder, onion powder, and 1 teaspoon of garlic powder. Mix gently with the hands until combined. 4. Form the mixture into 1½-inch balls. 5. Spray the meatballs with oil. Install the crisper plate in both baskets, place the meatballs in a single layer in the baskets, and insert the baskets into the unit. Select Zone 1 and select AIR FRY. Then set the temperature to 400°F and set the time to 5 minutes. Select MATCH COOK to match the Settings in Zone 2 with those in Zone 1. Select START/PAUSE to begin. Flip the meatballs and spray them with more oil. Cook for 4 to 7 minutes more, until an instant-read thermometer reads 165°F. 6. While the meatballs cook, place the ketchup, apple cider vinegar, mustard, and brown sugar substitute in a small saucepan over medium heat. Bring to a simmer and continue to cook for 5 minutes. Reduce the heat to low and add the remaining 1 teaspoon of garlic powder, remaining 1½ teaspoons of smoked paprika, liquid smoke, and ½ teaspoon of salt. Cook for 5 minutes more and stir occasionally, until thickened. 7. Once cooking has finished, toss the meatballs with the sauce and serve warm.
Per Serving: Calories 214; Fat 10. 63g; Sodium 453mg; Carbs 6. 16g; Fiber 1. 3g; Sugar 2. 8g; Protein 24. 04g

Cheesy Chicken Kiev

Prep Time: 25 minutes | Cook Time: 18 minutes | Serves: 8

½ cup (1 stick) unsalted butter, at room temperature
1 teaspoon minced garlic
2 tablespoons chopped fresh parsley
½ teaspoon freshly ground black pepper
2 pounds boneless, skinless chicken breasts
Sea salt
¾ cup finely ground blanched almond flour
¾ cup grated Parmesan cheese
⅛ teaspoon cayenne pepper
2 large eggs
Avocado oil spray

1. In a medium bowl, combine the butter, parsley, garlic, and black pepper. Form the mixture into a log and wrap it tightly with plastic wrap or parchment paper. Refrigerate for at least 2 hours until firm. 2. Place the chicken breasts in between two pieces of plastic wrap or a zip-top bag. Use a meat mallet or heavy skillet to pound the chicken to an even ¼-inch thickness. 3. Place a pat of butter in the center of each chicken breast and wrap the chicken tightly around the butter from the long side, tucking in the short sides as you go. Secure with toothpicks. Season the outside of the chicken with salt. Wrap the stuffed chicken tightly with plastic wrap and refrigerate at least 2 hours or overnight. 4. Combine the Parmesan cheese, almond flour, and cayenne pepper in a shallow bowl. 5. In another shallow bowl, beat the eggs. 6. Dip each chicken piece in the eggs and coat it in the almond flour mixture, using your fingers to press the breading gently into the chicken. 7. Spray the chicken with oil. Install the crisper plate in both baskets, place the chicken in a single layer in the baskets, and insert the baskets into the unit. Select Zone 1 and select AIR FRY. Then set the temperature to 350°F and set the time to 8 minutes. Select MATCH COOK to match the Settings in Zone 2 with those in Zone 1. Select START/PAUSE to begin. Flip the chicken, then spray it again with oil. Cook for 6 to 10 minutes more, until an instant-read thermometer reads 165°F. 8. Once cooking has finished, serve.
Per Serving: Calories 405; Fat 25. 44g; Sodium 628mg; Carbs 27. 99g; Fiber 3. 1g; Sugar 6. 75g; Protein 17. 3g

Creamy Cheese Turkey Pot Pie

Prep Time: 20 minutes | Cook Time: 35 minutes | Serves: 8

¼ cup (4 tablespoons) unsalted butter
2 shallots, minced
1 cup mushrooms, chopped
2 celery stalks, chopped
1 teaspoon minced garlic
1 teaspoon sea salt
¼ teaspoon freshly ground black pepper

1¾ cups turkey broth or chicken broth
⅔ cup heavy (whipping) cream
2 ounces cream cheese
½ teaspoon xanthan gum
3 cups chopped cooked turkey
½ cup frozen baby peas (optional)
1 recipe Fathead Pizza Dough

1. Cook the butter over medium heat to melt in a large saucepan. Add the mushrooms, shallots, and celery. Cook for 5 minutes, stirring frequently. Add the garlic, pepper, and salt to cook for 1 minute more. 2. Stir in the broth, cream cheese, heavy cream, and xanthan gum. Bring to a simmer and cook for 1 minute, stirring constantly. Reduce the temperature to low and continue to cook for 5 minutes, stirring often, until thickened. 3. Stir in the turkey and peas, if using. 4. Divide the mixture among 8 individual ramekins. 5. Roll out the pizza dough between two sheets of parchment paper. Cut the dough into pieces large enough to cover each ramekin, and place them over the filling. Cut a slit or two in the top of each crust to vent with a sharp knife. 6. Install the crisper plate in both baskets, place the ramekins in the baskets, and insert the baskets into the unit. Select Zone 1 and select AIR FRY. Then set the temperature to 325°F and set the time to 23 minutes. Select MATCH COOK to match the Settings in Zone 2 with those in Zone 1. Select START/PAUSE to begin. Cook until the crusts are golden brown. 7. Once cooking has finished, serve.

Per Serving: Calories 255; Fat 16. 34g; Sodium 795mg; Carbs 11. 74g; Fiber 1. 8g; Sugar 2. 09g; Protein 15. 54g

Delicious Tex–Mex Chicken Roll–Ups

Prep Time: 10 minutes | Cook Time: 17 minutes | Serves: 8

2 pounds boneless, skinless chicken breasts or thighs
1 teaspoon chili powder
½ teaspoon smoked paprika
½ teaspoon ground cumin
Sea salt

Freshly ground black pepper
6 ounces Monterey Jack cheese, shredded
4 ounces canned diced green chilies
Avocado oil spray

1. Place the chicken in a large zip-top bag or between two pieces of plastic wrap. Using a meat mallet or heavy skillet, pound the chicken until it is about ¼ inch thick. 2. In a small bowl, combine the chili powder, pepper, smoked paprika, salt and cumin. Sprinkle both sides of the chicken with the seasonings. 3. Sprinkle the chicken with the Monterey Jack cheese, then the diced green chilies. 4. Roll up each piece of chicken from the long side, tucking in the ends as you go. Secure the roll-up with a toothpick. 5. Spray the outside of the chicken with avocado oil. Install the crisper plate in both baskets, place the chicken in a single layer in the baskets, and insert the baskets into the unit. Select Zone 1 and select AIR FRY. Then set the temperature to 350°F and set the time to 7 minutes. Select MATCH COOK to match the Settings in Zone 2 with those in Zone 1. Select START/PAUSE to begin. Flip and cook for another 7 to 10 minutes, until an instant-read thermometer reads 160°F. 6. Once cooking has finished, remove the chicken and let it rest for about 5 minutes before serving.

Per Serving: Calories 257; Fat 10. 96g; Sodium 978mg; Carbs 0. 98g; Fiber 0. 5g; Sugar 0. 15g; Protein 37. 45g

Spiced Turkey Breasts with Celery

Prep Time: 5 minutes | Cook Time: 30 minutes | Serves: 4

1 big turkey breast, skinless, boneless and sliced
4 garlic cloves, minced
3 tablespoons olive oil
4 celery stalks, roughly chopped

1 teaspoon turmeric powder
1 teaspoon cumin, ground
1 tablespoon smoked paprika
1 tablespoon garlic powder

1. Install the crisper plate in the basket. Put the turkey and the other ingredients in the basket and toss. Insert the basket into the unit. 2. Select Zone 1 and select AIR FRY. Then set the temperature to 380°F and set the time to 30 minutes. Select START/PAUSE to begin. 3. Once cooking has finished, divide everything between plates and serve.

Per Serving: Calories 171; Fat 13. 11g; Sodium 40mg; Carbs 4. 91g; Fiber 1. 4g; Sugar 0. 53g; Protein 9. 11g

Cheesy Jalapeño Popper Chicken

Prep Time: 10 minutes | Cook Time: 17 minutes | Serves: 8

2 pounds boneless, skinless chicken breasts or thighs
Sea salt
Freshly ground black pepper
8 ounces cream cheese, at room temperature

4 ounces Cheddar cheese, shredded
2 jalapeños, seeded and diced
1 teaspoon minced garlic
Avocado oil spray

1. Place the chicken in a large zip-top bag or between two pieces of plastic wrap. Using a meat mallet or heavy skillet, pound the chicken until it is about ¼-inch thick. Season both sides of the chicken with pepper and salt. 2. In a medium bowl, combine the jalapeños, cream cheese, Cheddar cheese, and garlic. Divide the mixture among the chicken pieces. Roll up each piece from the long side, tucking in the ends as you go. Secure with toothpicks. 3. Spray the outside of the chicken with oil. Install the crisper plate in both baskets, place the chicken in a single layer in the baskets, and insert the baskets into the unit. Select Zone 1 and select AIR FRY. Then set the temperature to 350°F and set the time to 7 minutes. Select MATCH COOK to match the Settings in Zone 2 with those in Zone 1. Select START/PAUSE to begin. Flip the chicken and cook for another 7 to 10 minutes, until an instant-read thermometer reads 160°F. 4. Once cooking has finished, serve.

Per Serving: Calories 315; Fat 16. 23g; Sodium 874mg; Carbs 27. 56g; Fiber 1. 9g; Sugar 8. 65g; Protein 14. 7g

Smoky Paprika Chicken Leg Quarters

Prep Time: 5 minutes | Cook Time: 27 minutes | Serves: 6

½ cup avocado oil
2 teaspoons smoked paprika
1 teaspoon sea salt
1 teaspoon garlic powder

½ teaspoon dried rosemary
½ teaspoon dried thyme
½ teaspoon freshly ground black pepper
2 pounds bone-in, skin-on chicken leg quarters

1. In a blender or small bowl, combine the avocado oil, salt, garlic powder, smoked paprika, rosemary, thyme, and black pepper. 2. Arrange the chicken in a shallow dish or large zip-top bag. Pour the marinade over the chicken, making sure all the legs are coated. Cover to let it marinate for at least 2 hours or overnight. 3. Install the crisper plate in both baskets, place the chicken in a single layer in the baskets, and insert the baskets into the unit. Select Zone 1 and select AIR FRY. Then set the temperature to 400°F and set the time to 15 minutes. Select MATCH COOK to match the Settings in Zone 2 with those in Zone 1. Select START/PAUSE to begin. Flip the chicken legs, then reduce the temperature to 350°F. Cook for 8 to 12 minutes more, until an instant-read thermometer reads 160°F when inserted into the thickest piece of chicken. 4. Once cooking has finished, allow to rest for 5 to 10 minutes before serving.

Per Serving: Calories 489; Fat 42. 4g; Sodium 515mg; Carbs 1. 24g; Fiber 0. 4g; Sugar 0. 09g; Protein 24. 98g

Crispy Buffalo Egg Rolls

Prep Time: 20 minutes | Cook Time: 9 minutes | Serves: 8

1 teaspoon water
1 tablespoon cornstarch
1 egg
2½ cups cooked chicken, diced or shredded (see opposite page)
⅓ cup chopped green onion
⅓ cup diced celery
⅓ cup buffalo wing sauce

8 egg roll wraps
Oil for misting or cooking spray
Blue Cheese Dip:
3 ounces cream cheese, softened
⅓ cup blue cheese, crumbled
1 teaspoon Worcestershire sauce
¼ teaspoon garlic powder
¼ cup buttermilk (or sour cream)

1. Mix water and cornstarch in a small bowl until dissolved. Add egg to beat well, and set aside. 2. In a medium size bowl, mix together chicken, green onion, celery, and buffalo wing sauce. 3. Divide chicken mixture evenly among 8 egg roll wraps, spooning ½ inch from one edge. 4. Moisten all edges of each wrap with beaten egg wash. 5. Fold the short ends over filling, then roll up tightly and press to seal edges. 6. Brush outside of wraps with egg wash, then spritz with oil or cooking spray. 7. Install the crisper plate in both baskets, place the egg rolls in the baskets, and insert the baskets into the unit. 8. Select Zone 1 and select AIR FRY. Then set the temperature to 390°F and set the time to 9 minutes. Select MATCH COOK to match the Settings in Zone 2 with those in Zone 1. Select START/PAUSE to begin. Cook until outside is brown and crispy. 9. While the rolls are cooking, prepare the Blue Cheese Dip. With a fork, mash together cream cheese and blue cheese. 10. Stir in remaining ingredients. 11. Dip should be just thick enough to slightly cling to egg rolls. If too thick, stir in buttermilk or milk 1 tablespoon at a time until the desired consistency reached. 12. Once cooking has finished, serve while hot with Blue Cheese Dip, more buffalo wing sauce, or both.
Per Serving: Calories 271; Fat 10. 06g; Sodium 490mg; Carbs 25. 43g; Fiber 1. 5g; Sugar 6. 52g; Protein 18. 69g

Simple Chicken for Filling

Prep Time: 5 minutes | Cook Time: 8 minutes | Serves: 3

1 pound chicken tenders, skinless and boneless
½ teaspoon ground cumin

½ teaspoon garlic powder
Cooking spray

1. Sprinkle raw chicken tenders with seasonings. 2. Spray the crisper plate lightly with cooking spray to prevent sticking. 3. Install the crisper plate in the basket, place the chicken in the basket, and insert the basket into the unit. 4. Select Zone 1 and select AIR FRY. Then set the temperature to 390°F and set the time to 4 minutes. Select START/PAUSE to begin. 5. Turn chicken strips over, and cook for another 4 minutes. Test for doneness. Thick tenders may require another minute or two. 6. Once cooking has finished, serve.
Per Serving: Calories 180; Fat 5. 17g; Sodium 114mg; Carbs 0. 55g; Fiber 0. 1g; Sugar 0. 02g; Protein 30. 89g

Sour–Sweet Duck Breasts

Prep Time: 5 minutes | Cook Time: 20 minutes | Serves: 2

2 duck breasts, boneless and skin scored
A pinch of salt and black pepper
¼ teaspoon cinnamon powder

4 tablespoons stevia
3 tablespoons balsamic vinegar

1. In a bowl, mix the duck breasts with the rest of the ingredients and rub well. 2. Install the crisper plate in the basket, put the duck breasts in the basket, and insert the basket into the unit. Select Zone 1 and select AIR FRY. Then set the temperature to 380°F and set the time to 10 minutes. Select START/PAUSE to begin. 3. Cook 10 minutes on each side. 4. Once cooking has finished, divide everything between plates and serve.
Per Serving: Calories 228; Fat 7. 08g; Sodium 682mg; Carbs 24. 75g; Fiber 0. 3g; Sugar 3. 6g; Protein 33. 14g

Savory Rack of Lamb with Sauce
Prep Time: 5 minutes | Cook Time: 15 minutes | Serves: 2

2 racks of lamb
1 bunch of fresh mint
Salt and pepper to taste

⅓ cup extra-virgin olive oil
1 tablespoon honey
2 garlic cloves

1. Place all the ingredients into a blender except the lamb. Puree into a sauce. 2. Make small cuts in lamb racks, from top between bones, and then tie rack into crown shape using kitchen twine. 3. Smear rack generously with sauce. 4. Install the crisper plate in the basket, place the lamb rack in the basket, and insert the basket into the unit. Select Zone 1 and select AIR FRY. Then set the temperature to 390°F and set the time to 15 minutes. Select START/PAUSE to begin. 5. Open the air fryer every 5 minutes to layer more sauce onto rack. 6. Once cooking has finished, serve with mashed potatoes and fresh vegetables.
Per Serving: Calories 362; Fat 25. 27g; Sodium 1547mg; Carbs 10. 38g; Fiber 0. 4g; Sugar 8. 66g; Protein 24. 23g

Simple Lamb Chops
Prep Time: 5 minutes | Cook Time: 12 minutes | Serves: 4

1 tablespoon + 2 tablespoons olive oil, divided
4 lamb chops
Pinch of black pepper

1 tablespoon dried thyme
1 garlic clove

1. Cook the garlic with 1 teaspoon olive oil for 10 minutes in a saucepan. 2. Combine thyme and pepper with rest of olive oil. 3. Squeeze the roasted garlic and stir into thyme and oil mixture. Brush mixture over lamb chops. 4. Install the crisper plate in the basket, place the lamb chops in the basket, and insert the basket into the unit. Select Zone 1 and select AIR FRY. Then set the temperature to 390°F and set the time to 12 minutes. Select START/PAUSE to begin. 5. Once cooking has finished, serve.
Per Serving: Calories 256; Fat 18. 07g; Sodium 89mg; Carbs 0. 76g; Fiber 0. 2g; Sugar 0. 01g; Protein 23. 12g

Garlicy Rack of Lamb with Macadamia Crust
Prep Time: 15 minutes | Cook Time: 35 minutes | Serves: 4

1 garlic clove, minced
1 ⅓ lbs. rack of lamb
1 tablespoon olive oil
Salt and pepper to taste
Macadamia Crust:

3-ounces macadamia nuts, raw and unsalted
1 egg, beaten
1 tablespoon fresh rosemary, chopped
1 tablespoon breadcrumbs

1. In a small mixing bowl, mix garlic with olive oil. Brush all over lamb and season with pepper and salt. 2. In the food processor, chop macadamia nuts and mix with breadcrumbs and rosemary. Be careful not to make the nuts into a paste. Stir in egg. Coat lamb with nut mixture. 3. Install the crisper plate in the basket, place the lamb in the basket, and insert the basket into the unit. Select Zone 1 and select AIR FRY. Then set the temperature to 220°F and set the time to 30 minutes. Select START/PAUSE to begin. 4. Raise the temperature to 390°F and cook for another 5 minutes. 5. Once cooking has finished, remove the meat and cover it with foil for 10 minutes. Serve warm.
Per Serving: Calories 453; Fat 33. 67g; Sodium 131mg; Carbs 5. 64g; Fiber 2. 2g; Sugar 1. 7g; Protein 34. 72g

Onion Pumpkin & Pork Empanadas
Prep Time: 15 minutes | Cook Time: 25 minutes | Serves: 4

2 tablespoons olive oil
1 package of 10 empanada discs
Black pepper to taste
1 teaspoon salt
½ teaspoon dried thyme
½ teaspoon cinnamon

1 red chili pepper, minced
3 tablespoons water
1½ cups pumpkin puree
1 lb. ground pork
½ onion, diced

1. In a saucepan, warm some olive oil. Fry the onions and pork for about 5 minutes. 2. Pour away the fat, then add pumpkin, salt, chili, cinnamon, water, thyme, and pepper. Stir well. Cook for 10 minutes to let flavors blend. Set aside to cool. 3. Open the packet of empanada discs and spread them out over the countertop. Add a couple of tablespoons of filling to each, brush the edges with water and then fold towards center, to form a Cornish pasty shape. 4. Brush olive oil and repeat with the rest. Install the crisper plate in the basket, place the empanadas in the basket, and insert the basket into the unit. Select Zone 1 and select AIR FRY. Then set the temperature to 370°F and set the time to 15 minutes. Select START/PAUSE to begin. Make sure to check often and turn as required. 5. Once cooking has finished, serve and enjoy!
Per Serving: Calories 627; Fat 52. 55g; Sodium 761mg; Carbs 10. 21g; Fiber 3. 6g; Sugar 2. 31g; Protein 32. 97g

Pork Chops Satay with Peanut Sauce
Prep Time: 15 minutes | Cook Time: 17 minutes | Serves: 4

1 teaspoon ground ginger
2 teaspoons hot pepper sauce
2 cloves garlic, crushed
3 tablespoons sweet soy sauce
3 ½ ounces unsalted peanuts, ground

¾ cup coconut milk
1 teaspoon ground coriander
2 tablespoons vegetable oil
14-ounces lean pork chops, in cubes of 1-inch

1. In a large mixing bowl, combine hot sauce, half garlic, ginger, oil and soy sauce. Place the meat into the mixture and leave for 15 minutes to marinate. 2. Install the crisper plate in both baskets, place the meat in the baskets, and insert the baskets into the unit. Select Zone 1 and select AIR FRY. Then set the temperature to 390°F and set the time to 12 minutes. Select MATCH COOK to match the Settings in Zone 2 with those in Zone 1. Select START/PAUSE to begin. 3. Turn over halfway through cook time. 4. For the peanut sauce, place the oil into a skillet and heat it up. Add the garlic and coriander to cook for 5 minutes and stir often. Add the coconut milk, soy sauce, peanuts, and hot pepper sauce to the pan and bring to boil. Stir often. 5. Once cooking has finished, remove the pork and pour sauce over it and serve warm.
Per Serving: Calories 564; Fat 43. 05g; Sodium 245mg; Carbs 13. 69g; Fiber 3. 8g; Sugar 6. 2g; Protein 33. 92g

Marjoram Country–Style Ribs
Prep Time: 10 minutes | Cook Time: 12 minutes | Serves: 4

4 country-style pork ribs, trimmed of excess fat
Salt and black pepper to taste
1 teaspoon dried marjoram
1 teaspoon garlic powder

1 teaspoon thyme
2 teaspoons dry mustard
3 tablespoons coconut oil
3 tablespoons cornstarch

1. Place ingredients in a bowl, except pork ribs. Soak the ribs in the mixture and rub in. 2. Install the crisper plate in both baskets, place the ribs in the baskets, and insert the baskets into the unit. Select Zone 1 and select AIR FRY. Then set the temperature to 400°F and set the time to 12 minutes. Select MATCH COOK to match the Settings in Zone 2 with those in Zone 1. Select START/PAUSE to begin. 3. Once cooking has finished, serve and enjoy!
Per Serving: Calories 396; Fat 21. 44g; Sodium 162mg; Carbs 7. 39g; Fiber 0. 5g; Sugar 0. 62g; Protein 41. 39g

Garlic Pork Loin with Potatoes

Prep Time: 10 minutes | Cook Time: 25 minutes | Serves: 4

2 lbs. pork loin
½ teaspoon garlic powder
½ teaspoon red pepper flakes

½ teaspoon black pepper
2 large potatoes, chunked

1. Sprinkle the pork loin with garlic powder, parsley, salt, red pepper flakes, and pepper. 2. Install the crisper plate in both baskets, place the pork loin and potatoes in the baskets, and insert the baskets into the unit. Select Zone 1 and select AIR FRY. Then set the temperature to 370°F and set the time to 25 minutes. Select MATCH COOK to match the Settings in Zone 2 with those in Zone 1. Select START/PAUSE to begin. 3. Once cooking has finished, remove the pork loin and potatoes. Allow pork loin to cool before slicing and enjoy!
Per Serving: Calories 606; Fat 25. 29g; Sodium 155mg; Carbs 30. 05g; Fiber 4. 6g; Sugar 2. 42g; Protein 61. 4g

Lemony Pork with Pesto

Prep Time: 10 minutes | Cook Time: 20 minutes | Serves: 2

½ cup milk
1 egg
1 cup breadcrumbs
1 tablespoon parmesan cheese, grated
¼ bunch of thyme, chopped
1 teaspoon pine nuts
¼ cup semi-dried tomatoes

½ cup almond flour
2 pork cutlets
1 lemon, zested
Sea salt and black pepper to taste
6 basil leaves
1 tablespoon olive oil

1. Combine milk and egg in a bowl to whisk, then set aside. Mix breadcrumbs, thyme, lemon zest, salt, parmesan, and pepper in another bowl. 2. Add flour to another bowl. 3. Dip pork cutlet in flour, then into egg and milk mixture, and finally into breadcrumb mixture. 4. Spray the crisper plate with cooking spray. Install the crisper plate in the basket, place the pork in the basket, and insert the basket into the unit. Select Zone 1 and select AIR FRY. Then set the temperature to 360°F and set the time to 20 minutes. Select START/PAUSE to begin. Cook until golden and crisp. 5. Prepare the pesto: add the tomatoes, olive oil, pine nuts, and basil leaves into a food processor. Blend for 20 seconds. 6. When the pork is ready, serve with pesto and a salad of your choice.
Per Serving: Calories 757; Fat 35. 91g; Sodium 623mg; Carbs 50. 57g; Fiber 3. 8g; Sugar 11. 11g; Protein 56. 34g

Hoisin Garlic Pork Ribs

Prep Time: 10 minutes | Cook Time: 40 minutes | Serves: 6

4 garlic cloves, minced
1 tablespoon honey
2 lbs. pork ribs
2 tablespoons sesame oil

2 tablespoons ginger, minced
2 tablespoons hoisin sauce
2 tablespoons char Siu sauce
1 tablespoon soy sauce

1. Place the ingredients in a bowl except for meat and combine well. 2. Place the ribs in a bowl and pour the sauce over them and coat well. Place in the fridge for 4 hours. 3. Install the crisper plate in both baskets, place the ribs in the baskets, and insert the baskets into the unit. Select Zone 1 and select AIR FRY. Then set the temperature to 330°F and set the time to 40 minutes. Select MATCH COOK to match the Settings in Zone 2 with those in Zone 1. Select START/PAUSE to begin. 4. Increase the temperature to 350°F and cook for another 10 minutes. 5. Once cooking has finished, serve warm.
Per Serving: Calories 288; Fat 13. 76g; Sodium 271mg; Carbs 7. 32g; Fiber 0. 4g; Sugar 5. 13g; Protein 32. 02g

Sweet & Sour Pork Chunks
Prep Time: 10 minutes | Cook Time: 10 minutes | Serves: 4

1 cup cornstarch
½ teaspoon spice mix
¼ cup sweet and sour sauce
2 lbs. pork, chunked

3 tablespoons olive oil
2 large eggs, beaten
½ teaspoon sea salt
¼ teaspoon black pepper

1. In a bowl, combine spice mix, pepper, cornstarch, and salt. 2. In another bowl add beaten eggs. Coat pork chunks with cornstarch mixture, then dip in eggs and again into cornstarch. 3. Grease the crisper plate with olive oil. Install the crisper plate in both baskets, place the coated pork chunks in the baskets, and insert the baskets into the unit. Select Zone 1 and select AIR FRY. Then set the temperature to 340°F and set the time to 10 minutes. Select MATCH COOK to match the Settings in Zone 2 with those in Zone 1. Select START/PAUSE to begin. 4. Shake the basket halfway through the cook time. 5. Once cooking has finished, place the air fried pork chunks on serving dish and drizzle with sweet and sour sauce.

Per Serving: Calories 598; Fat 20. 49g; Sodium 524mg; Carbs 36. 24g; Fiber 0. 3g; Sugar 3. 39g; Protein 62. 64g

BBQ Sauce Pork Ribs
Prep Time: 10 minutes | Cook Time: 27 minutes | Serves: 2

1 lb. pork ribs
Salt and pepper to taste
½ cup BBQ sauce
1 teaspoon liquid Stevia

1 teaspoon spice mix
1 medium onion, chopped
1 tablespoon olive oil

1. Warm the oil in a pan over medium heat. Add onion to pan and sauté for 2 minutes. 2. Add stevia, spice mix, and BBQ sauce into pan and stir well. 3. Remove pan from heat and set aside. Season pork ribs with salt and pepper. 4. Install the crisper plate in the basket, place the pork ribs in the basket, and insert the basket into the unit. Select Zone 1 and select AIR FRY. Then set the temperature to 320°F and set the time to 10 minutes. Select START/PAUSE to begin. 5. Brush BBQ sauce on both sides of pork. Cook pork for another 15 minutes. 6. Once cooking has finished, cut into slices and serve.

Per Serving: Calories 429; Fat 19. 83g; Sodium 615mg; Carbs 11. 9g; Fiber 2. 4g; Sugar 6. 1g; Protein 49. 19g

Honey Soy Sauce Pork Chops
Prep Time: 10 minutes | Cook Time: 10 minutes | Serves: 6

6 pork loin chops
Pepper to taste
1 garlic clove
¼ teaspoon ground ginger

1 teaspoon balsamic vinegar
2 tablespoons soy sauce
2 tablespoons honey

1. Season pork chops with pepper. In a mixing bowl, add soy sauce, honey, garlic, vinegar, ground ginger, and mix well. 2. Add seasoned pork chops to bowl and coat well. Place pork chops in fridge for 2 hours. 3. Install the crisper plate in both baskets, place the marinated pork chops in the baskets, and insert the baskets into the unit. Select Zone 1 and select AIR FRY. Then set the temperature to 350°F and set the time to 10 minutes. Select MATCH COOK to match the Settings in Zone 2 with those in Zone 1. Select START/PAUSE to begin. Cook for 10 minutes. 4. Once cooking has finished, serve.

Per Serving: Calories 236; Fat 6. 82g; Sodium 169mg; Carbs 8. 18g; Fiber 0. 3g; Sugar 7. 3g; Protein 33. 84g

Garlicy Hoisin Pork Ribs

Prep Time: 10 minutes | Cook Time: 40 minutes | Serves: 2

1 lb. baby pork ribs
1 tablespoon olive oil
1 tablespoon hoisin sauce

½ tablespoon honey
½ tablespoon soy sauce
3 garlic cloves, minced

1. Add the ingredients in a bowl and mix well. Place the marinated ribs in fridge for 2 hours. 2. Install the crisper plate in the basket, put the marinated ribs in the basket, and insert the basket into the unit. Select Zone 1 and select AIR FRY. Then set the temperature to 320°F and set the time to 40 minutes. Select START/PAUSE to begin. 3. Once cooking has finished, serve.
Per Serving: Calories 429; Fat 20. 56g; Sodium 342mg; Carbs 10. 33g; Fiber 0. 4g; Sugar 7. 31g; Protein 47. 93g

Basil Cheese Pork Balls

Prep Time: 10 minutes | Cook Time: 15 minutes | Serves: 8

2 teaspoons Dijon mustard
5 basil leaves, chopped
Salt and pepper to taste
2 tablespoons cheddar cheese, grated

4 garlic cloves, minced
1 small apple, chopped
1 large onion, chopped
1 1b. pork, minced

1. Add the onion, minced pork, and apple into the mixing bowl and stir. Add the mustard, honey, cheese, basil, pepper, garlic, salt and mix well. 2. Make the small balls from the mixture. 3. Install the crisper plate in both baskets, put the small balls in the baskets, and insert the baskets into the unit. Select Zone 1 and select AIR FRY. Then set the temperature to 400°F and set the time to 15 minutes. Select MATCH COOK to match the Settings in Zone 2 with those in Zone 1. Then select START/PAUSE to begin. 4. Once cooking has finished, serve.
Per Serving: Calories 169; Fat 8. 75g; Sodium 92mg; Carbs 5. 53g; Fiber 0. 9g; Sugar 3. 06g; Protein 16. 72g

Delicious Pork Loin with Sweet Potatoes

Prep Time: 10 minutes | Cook Time: 25 minutes | Serves: 8

2 lbs. pork loin
2 large Sweet potatoes, diced
1 teaspoon salt

1 teaspoon pepper
½ teaspoon garlic powder
½ teaspoon parsley flakes

1. Add all the ingredients into the mixing bowls and mix well. 2. Install the crisper plate in both baskets, put the bowls with pork and sweet potato mixture in the baskets, and insert the baskets into the unit. Select Zone 1 and select AIR FRY. Then set the temperature to 350°F and set the time to 25 minutes. Select MATCH COOK to match the Settings in Zone 2 with those in Zone 1. Then select START/PAUSE to begin. 3. Once cooking has finished, carve up the pork into slices and serve with sweet potatoes.
Per Serving: Calories 280; Fat 12. 62g; Sodium 370mg; Carbs 10g; Fiber 1. 6g; Sugar 3. 21g; Protein 30. 09g

Homemade Pork Chops

Prep Time: 10 minutes | Cook Time: 22 minutes | Serves: 4

1 lb. pork chops, chopped
¾ cup cornstarch
½ teaspoon sea salt
¼ teaspoon black pepper
1 egg white

Stir Fry:
2 tablespoons olive oil
½ teaspoon sea salt
¼ teaspoon black pepper
2 scallions, sliced

1. Spray the crisper plate with cooking spray. 2. Beat the egg white with pepper and salt in a mixing bowl until foamy. Add the pork chop to the egg mixture and set aside for 20 minutes. Coat the marinated pork chops with cornstarch. 3. Install the crisper plate in the basket, put the pork chops in the basket, and insert the basket into the unit. Select Zone 1 and select AIR FRY. Then set the temperature to 360°F and set the time to 12 minutes. Select START/PAUSE to begin. 4. Shake the basket halfway through. Flip pork chops over and cook at 400°F for an additional 6 minutes. 5. Heat the olive oil in a pan over medium heat. Add, pepper, scallions, and salt into the pan and cook for about 1 minute. 6. When cooking is up, add the air fried pork chop pieces into the pan and toss to coat. Serve hot.
Per Serving: Calories 396; Fat 19. 34g; Sodium 661mg; Carbs 22. 74g; Fiber 0. 5g; Sugar 0. 24g; Protein 30. 18g

Garlic Tomato Pork

Prep Time: 10 minutes | Cook Time: 22 minutes | Serves: 4

¾ lb. pork, chunked
1 slice of pineapple, cut into pieces
1 medium tomato, chopped
2 tablespoons oyster sauce
2 tablespoons tomato sauce
1 tablespoon Worcestershire sauce

1 medium onion, sliced
1 tablespoon garlic, minced
1 teaspoon olive oil
Almond flour
1 egg, beaten
1 tablespoon liquid Stevia

1. Dip the pork pieces in the egg and coat with the flour. 2. Install the crisper plate in the basket, put the pork pieces in the basket, and insert the basket into the unit. Select Zone 1 and select AIR FRY. Then set the temperature to 250°F and set the time to 20 minutes. Select START/PAUSE to begin. 3. Heat the oil in a pan over medium heat. Place in the onion and garlic and cook for 2 minutes. Place all remaining ingredients into the pan and stir. 4. Once cooking has finished, add the pork to pan and stir well. Serve hot!
Per Serving: Calories 182; Fat 8. 51g; Sodium 1387mg; Carbs 9. 08g; Fiber 1. 1g; Sugar 5. 33g; Protein 17. 7g

Cheesy Mustard Pork Balls

Prep Time: 10 minutes | Cook Time: 14 minutes | Serves: 4

¾ lb. minced pork
Salt and pepper to taste
1 small onion, diced
1 teaspoon mustard

1 teaspoon honey
1 teaspoon garlic, minced
1 tablespoon cheddar cheese, grated

1. Place the ingredients into a mixing bowl and combine well. 2. Spray the crisper plate with cooking spray. Make some balls from the mixture. Install the crisper plate in the basket, put pork balls in the basket, and insert the basket into the unit. Select Zone 1 and select AIR FRY. Then set the temperature to 400°F and set the time to 14 minutes. Select START/PAUSE to begin. 3. Once cooking has finished, serve.
Per Serving: Calories 138; Fat 6. 12g; Sodium 1576mg; Carbs 5. 73g; Fiber 0. 5g; Sugar 4. 02g; Protein 15. 82g

Savory–Sweet Pork Roast

Prep Time: 10 minutes | Cook Time: 15 minutes | Serves: 4

2 lbs. pork shoulder, chopped
½ tablespoon salt
⅓ cup soy sauce

1 tablespoon honey
1 tablespoon liquid Stevia

1. Put all the ingredients into a mixing bowl and combine well. Place the marinated pork in fridge for 2 hours. 2. Spray the crisper plates with cooking spray. Install the crisper plate in both baskets, put the marinated pork pieces in the baskets, and insert the baskets into the unit. Select Zone 1 and select AIR FRY. Then set the temperature to 400°F and set the time to 10 minutes. Select MATCH COOK to match the Settings in Zone 2 with those in Zone 1. Then select START/PAUSE to begin. 3. Increase the temperature to 400°F and cook for an additional 5 minutes. 4. Once cooking has finished, serve.
Per Serving: Calories 378; Fat 16. 88g; Sodium 1338mg; Carbs 9. 66g; Fiber 0. 4g; Sugar 8. 37g; Protein 44. 06g

Garlic BBQ Pork Ribs

Prep Time: 10 minutes | Cook Time: 30 minutes | Serves: 2

2 garlic cloves, chopped
1 lb. pork ribs, chunked
3 tablespoons BBQ sauce
1 tablespoon honey

½ teaspoon mix spice
1 teaspoon sesame oil
Salt and black pepper to taste
1 teaspoon soy sauce

1. Combine the soy sauce, garlic, salt, sesame oil, pepper, mix spice, BBQ sauce, honey in a mixing bowl. Add the pork ribs in the bowl and mix well. Place the marinated pork into the fridge for 2 hours. 2. Install the crisper plate in the basket, put the marinated pork ribs in the basket, and insert the basket into the unit. Select Zone 1 and select AIR FRY. Then set the temperature to 350°F and set the time to 15 minutes. Select START/PAUSE to begin. 3. Toss the ribs over and cook for an additional 15 minutes. 4. Once cooking has finished, serve.
Per Serving: Calories 339; Fat 15. 63g; Sodium 385mg; Carbs 14. 34g; Fiber 1g; Sugar 11. 4g; Protein 48. 36g

Lemony Pork Belly Roast

Prep Time: 10 minutes | Cook Time: 80 minutes | Serves: 4

1½ lbs. of pork belly roast
1 teaspoon white pepper
1½ teaspoons rosemary
For Rubbing on Skin Only:
½ a teaspoon salt

1½ teaspoons five-spice
2 teaspoons garlic and onion seasoning

2 tablespoons lemon juice

1. Wash the pork belly under running water and pat it dry. 2. In a large-sized pot, boil some water and blanch the pork belly for about 12 minutes. Pat dry with kitchen paper towel. Let it air-dry for about 3 hours. 3. Prepare the rub: Mix all the ingredients except the lemon juice. Turn the pork belly around and make 3-4 straight cuts into the meat, about ½ an inch deep. 4. Massage dry rub all over meat. Turn it over and rub the salt on surface of skin and squeeze the lemon all over it. 5. Install the crisper plate in the basket, put the pork in the basket, and insert the basket into the unit. Select Zone 1 and select AIR FRY. Then set the temperature to 350°F and set the time to 30 minutes. Then select START/PAUSE to begin. 6. Then turn over to other side and cook for another 30 minutes. 7. Increase the temperature to 355°F and cook for another 20 minutes. 8. When cooking is up, serve warm.
Per Serving: Calories 335; Fat 15. 14g; Sodium 370mg; Carbs 1. 91g; Fiber 0. 3g; Sugar 0. 26g; Protein 45. 22g

Crunchy Cheese Meatballs

Prep Time: 10 minutes | Cook Time: 20 minutes | Serves: 4

¾ lb. ground pork
2 tablespoons mozzarella cheese, cubed
Salt and pepper to taste
3 tablespoons breadcrumbs

½ tablespoon Italian herbs
1 onion, chopped
1 egg

1. Place the ingredients in a bowl and mix well. Place the marinated mixture into the fridge for 1 hour. 2. Spray the crisper plate with cooking spray. Make small meatballs from the mixture. 3. Install the crisper plate in the basket, put the meatballs in the basket, and insert the basket into the unit. Select Zone 1 and select AIR FRY. Then set the temperature to 350°F and set the time to 20 minutes. Select START/PAUSE to begin. 4. Shake the basket halfway through the cook time. 5. Once cooking has finished, serve and enjoy!
Per Serving: Calories 329; Fat 20. 99g; Sodium 822mg; Carbs 8. 05g; Fiber 0. 9g; Sugar 2. 66g; Protein 25. 69g

Crispy Pork Chops

Prep Time: 10 minutes | Cook Time: 15 minutes | Serves: 2

2 pork chops
½ cup breadcrumbs
1 tablespoon olive oil

1 egg, beaten
1 tablespoon almond flour
Salt and pepper to taste

1. Season the pork chops with the pepper and salt. Add the flour to mixing bowl. 2. In another small bowl, add the beaten egg. In a third bowl, combine the breadcrumbs with olive oil. Coat the pork chops with flour, dip in the egg, and coat with the breadcrumbs. 3. Install the crisper plate in the basket, put the chops in the basket, and insert the basket into the unit. Select Zone 1 and select AIR FRY. Then set the temperature to 400°F and set the time to 10 minutes. Select START/PAUSE to begin. 4. Flip the chops over and cook on the other side for an additional 5 minutes. 5. Once cooking has finished, serve warm.
Per Serving: Calories 532; Fat 27. 97g; Sodium 1478mg; Carbs 20. 46g; Fiber 1. 6g; Sugar 1. 79g; Protein 46. 82g

Buttered Tenderloin Steaks with Mushrooms

Prep Time: 10 minutes | Cook Time: 20 minutes | Serves: 2

1½ pounds tenderloin steaks
2 tablespoons butter, melted
1 teaspoon garlic powder
½ teaspoon mustard powder

1 teaspoon cayenne pepper
Sea salt and ground black pepper, to taste
½ pound cremini mushrooms, sliced

1. Toss the beef with 1 tablespoon of the butter and spices. 2. Install the crisper plate in the basket, put the beef in the basket, and insert the basket into the unit. Select Zone 1 and select AIR FRY. Then set the temperature to 400°F and set the time to 10 minutes. Select START/PAUSE to begin. 3. Turn it over halfway through the cooking time. 4. Add in the mushrooms along with the remaining 1 tablespoon of the butter. Continue to cook an additional 5 minutes. 5. Once cooking has finished, serve warm. Bon appétit!
Per Serving: Calories 675; Fat 36. 18g; Sodium 887mg; Carbs 5. 8g; Fiber 1. 7g; Sugar 2. 4g; Protein 79. 52g

Spicy Pork Roast

Prep Time: 5 minutes | Cook Time: 55 minutes | Serves: 4

1½ pounds center-cut pork roast
1 tablespoon olive oil
Sea salt and freshly ground black pepper, to taste
1 teaspoon garlic powder

1 teaspoon hot paprika
½ teaspoon dried parsley flakes
½ teaspoon dried rosemary

1. Install the crisper plate in the basket. Place all ingredients in a lightly greased basket. Insert the basket into the unit. 2. Select Zone 1 and select AIR FRY. Then set the temperature to 360°F and set the time to 55 minutes. Select START/PAUSE to begin. 3. Turn them over halfway through the cooking time. 4. Once cooking has finished, serve warm and enjoy!
Per Serving: Calories 386; Fat 19. 15g; Sodium 744mg; Carbs 1. 27g; Fiber 0. 4g; Sugar 0. 08g; Protein 49. 3g

Homemade Pork Loin Chops

Prep Time: 5 minutes | Cook Time: 20 minutes | Serves: 4

1 pound pork loin chops
1 tablespoon olive oil

Sea salt and ground black pepper, to taste
1 tablespoon smoked paprika

1. Install the crisper plate in the basket. Place all ingredients in a lightly greased basket. Insert the basket into the unit. 2. Select Zone 1 and select AIR FRY. Then set the temperature to 400°F and set the time to 15 minutes. Select START/PAUSE to begin. 3. Cook the pork loin chops and turn them over halfway through the cooking time. 4. Once cooking has finished, serve. Bon appétit!
Per Serving: Calories 273; Fat 16. 15g; Sodium 645mg; Carbs 1. 29g; Fiber 0. 7g; Sugar 0. 18g; Protein 29. 34g

Chili Garlic Pork Spareribs

Prep Time: 5 minutes | Cook Time: 35 minutes | Serves: 4

2 pounds pork spareribs
1 teaspoon coarse sea salt
⅓ teaspoon freshly ground black pepper
1 tablespoon brown sugar

1 teaspoon cayenne pepper
1 teaspoon garlic powder
1 teaspoon mustard powder

1. Install the crisper plates in the baskets. Place all ingredients in the lightly greased baskets. Insert the baskets into the unit. 2. Select Zone 1 and select AIR FRY. Then set the temperature to 350°F and set the time to 35 minutes. Select MATCH COOK to match the Settings in Zone 2 with those in Zone 1. Select START/PAUSE to begin. 3. Cook the pork ribs chops and turn them over halfway through the cooking time. 4. Once cooking has finished, serve. Bon appétit!
Per Serving: Calories 313; Fat 9. 34g; Sodium 707mg; Carbs 3. 05g; Fiber 0. 3g; Sugar 2. 03g; Protein 51. 04g

Garlic Tomato Pork Belly

Prep Time: 5 minutes | Cook Time: 17 minutes | Serves: 6

1½ pounds pork belly, cut into pieces
¼ cup tomato sauce
1 tablespoon tamari sauce

2 tablespoons dark brown sugar
1 teaspoon garlic, minced
Sea salt and ground black pepper, to season

1. Install the crisper plate in the basket. Toss all ingredients in the lightly greased basket. Insert the basket into the unit. 2. Select Zone 1 and select AIR FRY. Then set the temperature to 400°F and set the time to 17 minutes. Select START/PAUSE to begin. 3. Cook the pork belly and shake the basket halfway through the cooking time. 4. Once cooking has finished, serve. Bon appétit!

Per Serving: Calories 617; Fat 60. 2g; Sodium 750mg; Carbs 6. 08g; Fiber 1. 5g; Sugar 3. 49g; Protein 11. 28g

Easy Garlic Pork Ribs

Prep Time: 10 minutes | Cook Time: 40 minutes | Serves: 2

1lb. baby pork ribs
1 tablespoon olive oil
1 tablespoon hoisin sauce

½ tablespoon honey
½ tablespoon soy sauce
3 garlic cloves, minced

1. Add the ingredients in a bowl and mix well. Place the marinated ribs in fridge for 2-hours. 2. Install the crisper plate in the basket, place the marinated ribs in the basket, and insert the basket into the unit. Select Zone 1 and select AIR FRY. Then set the temperature to 320°F and set the time to 40 minutes. Select START/PAUSE to begin. 3. Once cooking has finished, serve.

Per Serving: Calories 429; Fat 20. 56g; Sodium 342mg; Carbs 10. 33g; Fiber 0. 4g; Sugar 7. 31g; Protein 47. 93g

Cheesy Apple Pork Balls

Prep Time: 10 minutes | Cook Time: 15 minutes | Serves: 8

2 teaspoons Dijon mustard
5 basil leaves, chopped
Salt and pepper to taste
2 tablespoons cheddar cheese, grated

4 garlic cloves, minced
1 small apple, chopped
1 large onion, chopped
1 1b. pork, minced

1. Add the onion, minced pork, and apple into mixing bowl and stir. Add mustard, garlic, honey, pepper, cheese, basil, salt and mix well. 2. Make small balls from mixture. Install the crisper plate in the basket, place the balls in the basket, and insert the basket into the unit. Select Zone 1 and select AIR FRY. Then set the temperature to 400°F and set the time to 15 minutes. 3. Once cooking has finished, serve.

Per Serving: Calories 113; Fat 3. 68g; Sodium 67mg; Carbs 5. 48g; Fiber 0. 9g; Sugar 3. 05g; Protein 14. 12g

Yummy Pork Loin with Sweet Potatoes

Prep Time: 10 minutes | Cook Time: 25 minutes | Serves: 8

2 lbs. pork loin
2 large Sweet potatoes, diced
1 teaspoon salt

1 teaspoon pepper
½ teaspoon garlic powder
½ teaspoon parsley flakes

1. Add all the ingredients into mixing bowl and mix well. 2. Install the crisper plate in both baskets, place the mixture in the baskets, and insert the baskets into the unit. Select Zone 1 and select AIR FRY. Then set the temperature to 350°F and set the time to 25 minutes. Select MATCH COOK to match the Settings in Zone 2 with those in Zone 1. Select START/PAUSE to begin. 3. Once cooking has finished, carve up the pork into slices and serve with sweet potatoes.

Per Serving: Calories 193; Fat 4. 68g; Sodium 363mg; Carbs 10g; Fiber 1. 6g; Sugar 3. 21g; Protein 26. 44g

Traditional Chinese Pork Roast

Prep Time: 10 minutes | Cook Time: 15 minutes | Serves: 4

2 lbs. pork shoulder, chopped
½ tablespoon salt
⅓ cup soy sauce

1 tablespoon honey
1 tablespoon liquid Stevia

1. Place all the ingredients into a mixing bowl and combine well. Place marinated pork in fridge for 2-hours. 2. Spray the crisper plate with cooking spray. Install the crisper plate in both baskets, place the marinated pork pieces in the baskets, and insert the baskets into the unit. Select Zone 1 and select AIR FRY. Then set the temperature to 350°F and set the time to 10 minutes. Select MATCH COOK to match the Settings in Zone 2 with those in Zone 1. Select START/PAUSE to begin. 3. Now increase the temperature to 400°F and cook for another 5 minutes. 4. Once cooking has finished, serve.

Per Serving: Calories 378; Fat 16. 88g; Sodium 1338mg; Carbs 9. 66g; Fiber 0. 4g; Sugar 8. 37g; Protein 44. 06g

Tomato & Onion Pork

Prep Time: 10 minutes | Cook Time: 22 minutes | Serves: 4

¾ lb. pork, chunked
1 slice of pineapple, cut into pieces
1 medium tomato, chopped
2 tablespoons oyster sauce
2 tablespoons tomato sauce
1 tablespoon Worcestershire sauce

1 medium onion, sliced
1 tablespoon garlic, minced
1 teaspoon olive oil
Almond flour
1 egg, beaten
1 tablespoon liquid Stevia

1. Dip pork pieces in egg and then coat with flour. 2. Install the crisper plate in the basket, place the pork pieces in the basket, and insert the basket into the unit. Select Zone 1 and select AIR FRY. Then set the temperature to 250°F and set the time to 20 minutes. Select START/PAUSE to begin. 3. Cook oil in pan over medium heat. Then add onion and garlic into pan and sauté for 2 minutes. Place all remaining ingredients into pan and stir. 4. Once cooking has finished, add pork to pan and stir well. Serve hot!

Per Serving: Calories 182; Fat 8. 51g; Sodium 1387mg; Carbs 9. 08g; Fiber 1. 1g; Sugar 5. 33g; Protein 17. 7g

Cheesy Pork Balls with Onion

Prep Time: 10 minutes | Cook Time: 14 minutes | Serves: 4

¾ lb. minced pork
Salt and pepper to taste
1 small onion, diced
1 teaspoon mustard

1 teaspoon honey
1 teaspoon garlic, minced
1 tablespoon cheddar cheese, grated

1. Place the ingredients into a mixing bowl and combine well. 2. Spray the crisper plate with cooking spray. Make some balls from mixture. 3. Install the crisper plate in the basket, place the balls in the basket, and insert the basket into the unit. Select Zone 1 and select AIR FRY. Then set the temperature to 400°F and set the time to 14 minutes. Select START/PAUSE to begin. and place them into basket. 4. Once cooking has finished, serve.

Per Serving: Calories 137; Fat 5. 93g; Sodium 997mg; Carbs 5. 72g; Fiber 0. 5g; Sugar 4. 01g; Protein 15. 93g

Pork Chops with Scallions

Prep Time: 10 minutes | Cook Time: 22 minutes | Serves: 4

1 lb. pork chops, chopped
¾ cup cornstarch
½ teaspoon sea salt
¼ teaspoon black pepper
1 egg white

2 tablespoons olive oil
½ teaspoon sea salt
¼ teaspoon black pepper
2 scallions, sliced

1. Spray the crisper plate with cooking spray. 2. Beat egg white with pepper and salt in a mixing bowl until foamy. Add pork chop to egg mixture and set aside for 20 minutes. Coat marinated pork chops with cornstarch. 3. Install the crisper plate in the basket, place the marinated pork chops in the basket, and insert the basket into the unit. Select Zone 1 and select AIR FRY. Then set the temperature to 360°F and set the time to 12 minutes. Select START/PAUSE to begin. 4. Shake the basket halfway through. Flip pork chops over and cook at 400°F for another 6 minutes. 5. Cook the olive oil in a pan over medium heat. Add jalapeno, pepper, scallions, and salt into pan and cook for about 1-minute. 6. Once cooking has finished, add air fried pork chop pieces into pan and toss to coat. Serve hot.

Per Serving: Calories 396; Fat 19. 34g; Sodium 661mg; Carbs 22. 74g; Fiber 0. 5g; Sugar 0. 24g; Protein 30. 18g

Spiced BBQ Pork Ribs

Prep Time: 10 minutes | Cook Time: 30 minutes | Serves: 2

2 garlic cloves, chopped
1 lb. pork ribs, chunked
3 tablespoons BBQ sauce
1 tablespoon honey

½ teaspoon mix spice
1 teaspoon sesame oil
Salt and black pepper to taste
1 teaspoon soy sauce

1. Combine soy sauce, pepper, garlic, salt, sesame oil, BBQ sauce, mix spice, honey in a mixing bowl. 2. Add pork ribs in bowl and mix well. Place marinated pork into fridge for 2 hours. 3. Install the crisper plate in the basket, place the marinated pork ribs in the basket, and insert the basket into the unit. Select Zone 1 and select AIR FRY. Then set the temperature to 350°F and set the time to 15 minutes. Select START/PAUSE to begin. 4. Toss ribs over and cook for another 15 minutes. 5. Once cooking has finished, serve.

Per Serving: Calories 399; Fat 15. 63g; Sodium 385mg; Carbs 14. 34g; Fiber 1g; Sugar 11. 4g; Protein 48. 36g

Spiced Pork Belly Roast

Prep Time: 10 minutes | Cook Time: 80 minutes | Serves: 4

1½ lbs. of pork belly roast
1 teaspoon white pepper
1½ teaspoons rosemary
1½ teaspoons five-spice

2 teaspoons garlic and onion seasoning
For Rubbing on Skin Only:
½ a teaspoon salt
2 tablespoons lemon juice

1. Wash the pork belly under running water and pat it dry. 2. In a large-sized pot, boil some water and blanch the pork belly for about 12 minutes. 3. Pat dry with kitchen paper towel. Let it air-dry for about 3 hours. 4. Prepare the rub. Combine all the ingredients except the lemon juice. Turn the pork belly around and make 3-4 straight cuts into the meat, about ½ an inch deep (so drier rub will get into the meat). Massage dry rub all over meat. Turn it over and rub salt on surface of skin and squeeze lemon all over it. 5. Install the crisper plate in the basket, place the pork belly in the basket, and insert the basket into the unit. Select Zone 1 and select AIR FRY. Then set the temperature to 320°F and set the time to 30 minutes. Select START/PAUSE to begin. 6. Then turn over to other side and cook for another 30 minutes. Increase the temperature to 355°F and cook for another 20 minutes. 7. Once cooking has finished, serve warm.
Per Serving: Calories 194; Fat 3. 83g; Sodium 382mg; Carbs 1. 91g; Fiber 0. 3g; Sugar 0. 26g; Protein 35. 86g

Herbed Cheese Meatballs

Prep Time: 10 minutes | Cook Time: 20 minutes | Serves: 4

¾ lb. ground pork
2 tablespoons mozzarella cheese, cubed
Salt and pepper to taste
3 tablespoons breadcrumbs

½ tablespoon Italian herbs
1 onion, chopped
1 egg

1. Place the ingredients in a bowl and mix well. Place marinated mixture into fridge for 1-hour. 2. Spray the crisper plate with cooking spray. Make small meatballs from mixture. 3. Install the crisper plate in the basket, place the meatballs in the basket, and insert the basket into the unit. Select Zone 1 and select AIR FRY. Then set the temperature to 350°F and set the time to 20 minutes. Select START/PAUSE to begin. 4. Shake the basket halfway through the cook time. 5. Once cooking has finished, serve and enjoy!
Per Serving: Calories 343; Fat 22. 01g; Sodium 251mg; Carbs 8. 21g; Fiber 0. 9g; Sugar 2. 78g; Protein 26. 55g

Creamy Cheese Shrimps

Prep Time: 15 minutes | Cook Time: 5 minutes | Serves: 4

14 oz shrimps, peeled
2 eggs, beaten
¼ cup heavy cream
1 teaspoon salt

1 teaspoon ground black pepper
4 oz Monterey jack cheese, shredded
5 tablespoons coconut flour
1 tablespoon lemon juice, for garnish

1. In the mixing bowl, mix up salt, heavy cream, and ground black pepper. Add eggs and whisk the mixture until homogenous. 2. After this, mix up coconut flour with Monterey jack cheese. 3. Dip the shrimps in the heavy cream mixture and coat in the coconut flour mixture. Then dip the shrimps in the egg mixture again and coat in the coconut flour. 4. Install the crisper plate in both baskets, place the shrimps in one layer in the baskets, and insert the baskets into the unit. Select Zone 1 and select AIR FRY. Then set the temperature to 400°F and set the time to 5 minutes. Select MATCH COOK to match the Settings in Zone 2 with those in Zone 1. Select START/PAUSE to begin. 5. Once cooking has finished, sprinkle the bang-bang shrimps with lemon juice.
Per Serving: Calories 254; Fat 14. 03g; Sodium 924mg; Carbs 1. 98g; Fiber 0. 4g; Sugar 1. 02g; Protein 30. 02g

Lime Cream Salmon

Prep Time: 5 minutes | Cook Time: 20 minutes | Serves: 4

4 salmon fillets, boneless
¼ cup coconut cream
1 teaspoon lime zest, grated
⅓ cup heavy cream

¼ cup lime juice
½ cup coconut, shredded
A pinch of salt and black pepper

1. In a bowl, mix all the ingredients except the salmon and whisk. 2. Install the crisper plate in the basket, place the fish in the basket, drizzling the coconut sauce all over, and insert the basket into the unit. Select Zone 1 and select AIR FRY. Then set the temperature to 360°F and set the time to 20 minutes. Select START/PAUSE to begin. 3. Once cooking has finished, divide between plates and serve.
Per Serving: Calories 352; Fat 21. 15g; Sodium 112mg; Carbs 4. 83g; Fiber 0. 9g; Sugar 1. 91g; Protein 35. 08g

Coconut Catfish Bites

Prep Time: 10 minutes | Cook Time: 10 minutes | Serves: 4

¼ cup coconut flakes
3 tablespoons coconut flour
1 teaspoon salt

3 eggs, beaten
10 oz catfish fillet
Cooking spray

1. Cut the catfish fillet on the small pieces (nuggets) and sprinkle with salt. 2. After this, dip the catfish pieces in the egg and coat in the coconut flour. Then dip the fish pieces in the egg again and coat in the coconut flakes. 3. Install the crisper plate in both baskets, place the catfish nuggets in the baskets, and insert the baskets into the unit. Select Zone 1 and select AIR FRY. Then set the temperature to 385°F and set the time to 6 minutes. Select MATCH COOK to match the Settings in Zone 2 with those in Zone 1. Select START/PAUSE to begin. 4. Then flip the nuggets on another side and cook them for 4 minutes more. 5. Once cooking has finished, serve.
Per Serving: Calories 198; Fat 11. 49g; Sodium 715mg; Carbs 3. 94g; Fiber 0. 7g; Sugar 2. 74g; Protein 18. 58g

Parmesan Cod Fillets
Prep Time: 10 minutes | Cook Time: 14 minutes | Serves: 4

1 cup parmesan, grated
4 cod fillets, boneless

Salt and black pepper to the taste
1 tablespoon mustard

1. In a bowl, mix the parmesan with salt, pepper and mustard to stir. Spread this over the cod. 2. Install the crisper plate in the basket, place the fish in the basket, and insert the basket into the unit. Select Zone 1 and select AIR FRY. Then set the temperature to 370°F and set the time to 7 minutes. Select START/PAUSE to begin. Cook for 7 minutes on each side. 3. Once cooking has finished, divide between plates and serve with a side salad.

Per Serving: Calories 161; Fat 1. 63g; Sodium 625mg; Carbs 9. 29g; Fiber 0. 3g; Sugar 0. 91g; Protein 26. 08g

Coconut Cream Salmon
Prep Time: 10 minutes | Cook Time: 7 minutes | Serves: 2

8 oz salmon fillet
2 tablespoons coconut flakes
1 tablespoon coconut cream
½ teaspoon salt

½ teaspoon ground turmeric
½ teaspoon onion powder
1 teaspoon nut oil

1. Cut the salmon fillet into halves and sprinkle with ground turmeric, salt, and onion powder. 2. After this, dip the fish fillets in the coconut cream and coat in the coconut flakes. Sprinkle the salmon fillets with nut oil. 3. Install the crisper plate in both baskets, place the salmon fillets in the baskets, and insert the baskets into the unit. Select Zone 1 and select AIR FRY. Then set the temperature to 380°F and set the time to 7 minutes. Select MATCH COOK to match the Settings in Zone 2 with those in Zone 1. Select START/PAUSE to begin. 4. Once cooking has finished, serve.

Per Serving: Calories 247; Fat 14. 5g; Sodium 1088mg; Carbs 4. 23g; Fiber 1g; Sugar 2. 01g; Protein 23. 97g

Savory Salmon Fillets
Prep Time: 10 minutes | Cook Time: 15 minutes | Serves: 4

3 tablespoons parsley, chopped
4 salmon fillets, boneless
¼ cup ghee, melted

2 garlic cloves, minced
4 shallots, chopped
Salt and black pepper to the taste

1. Heat up a pan with the ghee over medium-high heat, add the garlic, salt, shallots, pepper and the parsley, stir and cook for 5 minutes. 2. Add the salmon fillets and toss gently. 3. Install the crisper plate in the basket, place the salmon fillets in the basket, and insert the basket into the unit. Select Zone 1 and select AIR FRY. Then set the temperature to 380°F and set the time to 15 minutes. Select START/PAUSE to begin. 4. Once cooking has finished, divide between plates and serve.

Per Serving: Calories 611; Fat 28. 62g; Sodium 202mg; Carbs 3. 42g; Fiber 0. 6g; Sugar 1. 4g; Protein 80. 41g

Chili Tilapia

Prep Time: 15 minutes | Cook Time: 9 minutes | Serves: 2

1 chili pepper, chopped
1 teaspoon chili flakes
1 tablespoon sesame oil

½ teaspoon salt
10 oz tilapia fillet
¼ teaspoon onion powder

1. In the shallow bowl, mix up chili pepper, salt, chili flakes, and onion powder. Gently churn the mixture and add sesame oil. 2. After this, slice the tilapia fillet and sprinkle with chili mixture. Massage the fish with the help of the fingertips gently and leave for 10 minutes to marinate. 3. Install the crisper plate in both baskets, place the tilapia fillets in the baskets, and insert the baskets into the unit. Select Zone 1 and select AIR FRY. Then set the temperature to 390°F and set the time to 5 minutes. Select MATCH COOK to match the Settings in Zone 2 with those in Zone 1. Select START/PAUSE to begin. 4. Then flip the fish on another side and cook for 4 minutes more. 5. Once cooking has finished, serve.
Per Serving: Calories 210; Fat 9. 45g; Sodium 696mg; Carbs 3. 04g; Fiber 0. 9g; Sugar 1. 26g; Protein 29. 13g

Sweet Paprika Cod with Endives

Prep Time: 5 minutes | Cook Time: 20 minutes | Serves: 4

2 endives, shredded
2 tablespoons olive oil
Salt and black pepper to the taste

4 salmon fillets, boneless
½ teaspoon sweet paprika

1. In a pan, combine the fish with the rest of the ingredients and toss. 2. Install the crisper plate in the basket, place the fish Select Zone 1 and select AIR FRY. Then set the temperature to 350°F and set the time to 20 minutes. Select START/PAUSE to begin. in the basket, and insert the basket into the unit. 3. Flip the fish halfway. 4. Once cooking has finished, divide between plates and serve right away.
Per Serving: Calories 584; Fat 22. 25g; Sodium 256mg; Carbs 9. 82g; Fiber 8. 2g; Sugar 1. 25g; Protein 83. 23g

Lemony Salmon with Sesame

Prep Time: 10 minutes | Cook Time: 9 minutes | Serves: 6

18 oz salmon fillet
2 tablespoons swerve
1 tablespoon apple cider vinegar
6 teaspoons liquid aminos
1 teaspoon minced ginger

1 tablespoon sesame seeds
2 tablespoons lemon juice
½ teaspoon minced garlic
1 tablespoon avocado oil

1. Cut the salmon fillet on 8 servings and sprinkle with apple cider vinegar, lemon juice, minced ginger, minced garlic, and liquid aminos. Leave the fish for 10 to 15 minutes to marinate. 2. After this, sprinkle the fish with avocado oil. Install the crisper plate in both baskets, place the fish in the baskets, and insert the baskets into the unit. Select Zone 1 and select AIR FRY. Then set the temperature to 380°F and set the time to 7 minutes. Select MATCH COOK to match the Settings in Zone 2 with those in Zone 1. Select START/PAUSE to begin. 3. Then sprinkle them with swerve and sesame seeds and cook for 2 minutes more at 400°F. 4. Once cooking has finished, serve.
Per Serving: Calories 164; Fat 9. 42g; Sodium 369mg; Carbs 0. 81g; Fiber 0. 2g; Sugar 0. 15g; Protein 17. 95g

Lime Tuna Skewers

Prep Time: 5 minutes | Cook Time: 12 minutes | Serves: 4

1 pound tuna steaks, boneless and cubed
1 chili pepper, minced
4 green onions, chopped

2 tablespoons lime juice
A drizzle of olive oil
Salt and black pepper to the taste

1. In a bowl, mix all the ingredients and toss them. 2. Thread the tuna cubes on skewers. Install the crisper plate in the basket, place the skewers in the basket, and insert the basket into the unit. Select Zone 1 and select AIR FRY. Then set the temperature to 370°F and set the time to 12 minutes. Select START/PAUSE to begin. 3. Once cooking has finished, divide between plates and serve with a side salad.
Per Serving: Calories 134; Fat 2. 22g; Sodium 292mg; Carbs 6. 84g; Fiber 1. 6g; Sugar 4. 05g; Protein 23. 22g

Creamy Haddock Fillet

Prep Time: 10 minutes | Cook Time: 8 minutes | Serves: 4

1-pound haddock fillet
1 teaspoon cayenne pepper
1 teaspoon salt

1 teaspoon coconut oil
½ cup heavy cream

1. Grease the crisper plate with coconut oil. 2. Install the crisper plate in the basket, place the haddock fillet in the basket, and sprinkle it with cayenne pepper, salt, and heavy cream. Insert the basket into the unit. Select Zone 1 and select AIR FRY. Then set the temperature to 375°F and set the time to 8 minutes. Select START/PAUSE to begin. 3. Once cooking has finished, serve.
Per Serving: Calories 147; Fat 7. 26g; Sodium 829mg; Carbs 0. 67g; Fiber 0. 1g; Sugar 0. 47g; Protein 18. 87g

Garlicy Jalapeno Cod

Prep Time: 5 minutes | Cook Time: 14 minutes | Serves: 4

4 cod fillets, boneless
1 jalapeno, minced

1 tablespoon avocado oil
½ teaspoon minced garlic

1. In the shallow bowl, mix avocado oil, minced jalapeno, and minced garlic. 2. Install the crisper plate in the basket, place the cod fillets in one layer in the basket and top with minced jalapeno mixture. Insert the basket into the unit. Select Zone 1 and select AIR FRY. Then set the temperature to 365°F and set the time to 7 minutes. Select START/PAUSE to begin. Cook the fish for 7 minutes per side. 3. Once cooking has finished, serve.
Per Serving: Calories 282; Fat 18. 82g; Sodium 417mg; Carbs 8. 83g; Fiber 5. 4g; Sugar 1. 26g; Protein 19. 8g

Lime Sea Bass with Tomato and Okra

Prep Time: 5 minutes | Cook Time: 20 minutes | Serves: 4

4 sea bass fillets, boneless
A pinch of salt and black pepper
2 spring onions, chopped
Juice of 1 lime
1 garlic clove, minced

2 tomatoes, cubed
2 cups coconut cream
½ cup okra
A handful coriander, chopped
2 red chilies, minced

1. Put the coconut cream in a saucepan, add the garlic, spring onions, tomatoes, okra, lime juice, chilies and the coriander and toss. 2. Bring to a simmer and cook for 5 to 6 minutes. Add the fish and toss gently. 3. Install the crisper plate in both baskets, put the fish in the baskets, and insert the baskets into the unit. Select Zone 1 and select AIR FRY. Then set the temperature to 380°F and set the time to 15 minutes. Select MATCH COOK to match the Settings in Zone 2 with those in Zone 1. Then select START/PAUSE to begin. 4. Once cooking has finished, divide between plates and serve.

Per Serving: Calories 551; Fat 44. 58g; Sodium 138mg; Carbs 14. 77g; Fiber 4. 7g; Sugar 2. 84g; Protein 29. 55g

Chili Shrimp and Sausage Gumbo

Prep Time: 10 minutes | Cook Time: 12 minutes | Serves: 4

10 oz shrimps, peeled
5 oz smoked sausages, chopped
1 teaspoon olive oil
1 teaspoon ground black pepper
3 spring onions, diced

1 jalapeno pepper, chopped
½ cup chicken broth
1 teaspoon chili flakes
½ teaspoon dried cilantro
½ teaspoon salt

1. In the mixing bowl, mix up the smoked sausages, ground black pepper, and chili flakes. 2. Install the crisper plate in both baskets, put the smoked sausages in the baskets, and insert the baskets into the unit. Select Zone 1 and select AIR FRY. Then set the temperature to 400°F and set the time to 4 minutes. Select MATCH COOK to match the Settings in Zone 2 with those in Zone 1. Then select START/PAUSE to begin. 3. Meanwhile, in the mixing bowl, mix up the jalapeno pepper, onion, and salt. 4. Put the ingredients in the pan and sprinkle with olive oil. 5. After cooking for 4 minutes, remove the sausages from the basket. Put the onion in the basket and cook it for 2 minutes. 6. After this, add the smoked sausages, dried cilantro, and shrimps. Add chicken broth. Stir the ingredients gently and cook the meal for 6 minutes at 400°F. 7. Once cooking has finished, serve.

Per Serving: Calories 184; Fat 9. 31g; Sodium 788mg; Carbs 6. 04g; Fiber 2g; Sugar 0. 86g; Protein 21. 47g

Lime Coconut Clams

Prep Time: 5 minutes | Cook Time: 20 minutes | Serves: 4

15 small clams
1 tablespoon spring onions, chopped
Juice of 1 lime

10 ounces coconut cream
2 tablespoons cilantro, chopped
1 teaspoon olive oil

1. Heat up a saucepan with the oil over medium heat. Add the spring onions and sauté for 2 minutes. 2. Add the coconut cream, lime juice, and the cilantro, stir and cook for 2 minutes more. Add the clams and toss. 3. Install the crisper plate in both baskets, put the clams in the baskets, and insert the baskets into the unit. Select Zone 1 and select AIR FRY. Then set the temperature to 390°F and set the time to 15 minutes. Select MATCH COOK to match the Settings in Zone 2 with those in Zone 1. Then select START/PAUSE to begin. 4. Once cooking has finished, divide into bowls and serve hot.

Per Serving: Calories 56; Fat 1. 6g; Sodium 278mg; Carbs 4. 89g; Fiber 0. 9g; Sugar 2. 08g; Protein 5. 55g

Coconut Tilapia

Prep Time: 10 minutes | Cook Time: 12 minutes | Serves: 2

8 oz tilapia fillet
1 teaspoon coconut cream
1 teaspoon coconut flour
½ teaspoon salt

¼ teaspoon smoked paprika
½ teaspoon dried oregano
½ teaspoon coconut oil, melted
¼ teaspoon ground cumin

1. Rub the tilapia fillet with the ground cumin, smoked paprika, dried oregano, and salt. Then dip it in the coconut cream. Cut the tilapia fillet on 2 servings. 2. After this, sprinkle every tilapia fillet with coconut flour gently. 3. Sprinkle the crisper plates with coconut oil. Install the crisper plate in both baskets, put the tilapia fillets in the baskets, and insert the baskets into the unit. Select Zone 1 and select AIR FRY. Then set the temperature to 385°F and set the time to 6 minutes. Select MATCH COOK to match the Settings in Zone 2 with those in Zone 1. Then select START/PAUSE to begin. 4. Cook the fillets for 6 minutes from every side. 5. Once cooking has finished, serve.

Per Serving: Calories 130; Fat 4. 05g; Sodium 644mg; Carbs 0. 7g; Fiber 0. 3g; Sugar 0. 11g; Protein 22. 99g

Spicy Cod Fillets

Prep Time: 5 minutes | Cook Time: 15 minutes | Serves: 4

4 cod fillets, boneless
A pinch of salt and black pepper
1 tablespoon thyme, chopped
½ teaspoon black peppercorns
2 tablespoons olive oil

1 fennel, sliced
2 garlic cloves, minced
1 red bell pepper, chopped
2 teaspoons Italian seasoning

1. In a bowl, mix the fennel with bell pepper and the other ingredients except the fish fillets and toss. 2. Install the crisper plate in the basket, put the mixture in the basket, and add the fish on top. Insert the basket into the unit. Select Zone 1 and select AIR FRY. Then set the temperature to 380°F and set the time to 15 minutes. Select START/PAUSE to begin. 3. Once cooking has finished, divide between plates and serve.

Per Serving: Calories 160; Fat 7. 36g; Sodium 1048mg; Carbs 4. 46g; Fiber 1. 3g; Sugar 1. 65g; Protein 18. 45g

Creamy Coconut Cod Strips

Prep Time: 10 minutes | Cook Time: 6 minutes | Serves: 4

10 oz cod fillet
1 tablespoon coconut flour
1 tablespoon coconut flakes
1 egg, beaten

1 teaspoon ground turmeric
½ teaspoon salt
1 tablespoon heavy cream
1 teaspoon olive oil

1. Cut the cod fillets on the fries strips. After this, in the mixing bowl, mix up the ground turmeric, coconut flour, coconut flakes, and salt. 2. In the other bowl, mix up the egg and heavy cream. 3. After this, dip the fish fries in the egg mixture. Then coat them in the coconut flour mixture. Repeat the steps again. 4. Install the crisper plate in both baskets. Put the fish fries in the baskets in one layer and sprinkle them with olive oil. Insert the baskets into the unit. 5. Select Zone 1 and select AIR FRY. Then set the temperature to 400°F and set the time to 3 minutes. Select MATCH COOK to match the Settings in Zone 2 with those in Zone 1. Then select START/PAUSE to begin. 6. Cook the meal for 3 minutes. Then flip the fish fries on another side and cook for 3 minutes more. 7. Once cooking has finished, serve.

Per Serving: Calories 113; Fat 5. 62g; Sodium 540mg; Carbs 1. 69g; Fiber 0. 3g; Sugar 0. 88g; Protein 13. 28g

Chili Garlic Sea Bass

Prep Time: 5 minutes | Cook Time: 15 minutes | Serves: 4

4 sea bass fillets, boneless
4 garlic cloves, minced
Juice of 1 lime
1 cup veggie stock
A pinch of salt and black pepper

1 tablespoon black peppercorns, crushed
1-inch ginger, grated
4 lemongrass, chopped
4 small chilies, minced
1 bunch coriander, chopped

1. Combine all the ingredients except the fish in a blender and pulse well. Pour the mix in a pan, add the fish and toss well. 2. Install the crisper plate in the basket, put the fish in the basket, and insert the basket into the unit. Select Zone 1 and select AIR FRY. Then set the temperature to 380°F and set the time to 15 minutes. Select START/PAUSE to begin. 3. Once cooking has finished, divide between plates and serve.
Per Serving: Calories 196; Fat 3. 93g; Sodium 454mg; Carbs 12. 73g; Fiber 2. 2g; Sugar 2. 06g; Protein 26. 82g

Garlicky Buttery Haddock

Prep Time: 10 minutes | Cook Time: 16 minutes | Serves: 2

7 oz haddock fillet
2 tablespoons butter, melted
1 teaspoon minced garlic

½ teaspoon salt
1 teaspoon fresh parsley, chopped
½ teaspoon ground celery root

1. Cut the fish fillet on 2 servings. In the shallow bowl, mix up the butter and minced garlic. Then add the celery root, salt, and fresh parsley. 2. After this, carefully brush the fish fillets with the butter mixture. Then wrap every fillet in the foil. 3. Install the crisper plate in the basket, put the wrapped haddock fillets in the basket, and insert the basket into the unit. Select Zone 1 and select AIR FRY. Then set the temperature to 385°F and set the time to 16 minutes. Select START/PAUSE to begin. 4. Once cooking has finished, serve.
Per Serving: Calories 178; Fat 11. 98g; Sodium 885mg; Carbs 0. 53g; Fiber 0. 1g; Sugar 0. 04g; Protein 16. 43g

Spicy Shrimp Bowls

Prep Time: 5 minutes | Cook Time: 10 minutes | Serves: 4

2 pounds shrimp, peeled and deveined
A drizzle of olive oil
¼ cup chicken stock
1 tablespoon Italian seasoning

Salt and black pepper to the taste
1 teaspoon red pepper flakes, crushed
8 garlic cloves, crushed

1. Install the crisper plate greased with the oil in both baskets, put the shrimp and the rest of the ingredients in the baskets, tossing well, and insert the baskets into the unit. 2. Select Zone 1 and select AIR FRY. Then set the temperature to 390°F and set the time to 10 minutes. Select MATCH COOK to match the Settings in Zone 2 with those in Zone 1. Then select START/PAUSE to begin. 3. Once cooking has finished, divide into bowls and serve.
Per Serving: Calories 218; Fat 1. 69g; Sodium 1035mg; Carbs 4. 17g; Fiber 0. 6g; Sugar 0. 57g; Protein 46. 51g

Tasty Tarragon and Spring Onions Salmon
Prep Time: 15 minutes | Cook Time: 15 minutes | Serves: 4

12 oz salmon fillet
2 spring onions, chopped
1 tablespoon ghee, melted
1 teaspoon peppercorns

½ teaspoon salt
½ teaspoon ground black pepper
1 teaspoon tarragon
½ teaspoon dried cilantro

1. Cut the salmon fillet on 4 servings. 2. Then make the parchment pockets and place the fish fillets in the parchment pockets. Sprinkle the salmon with salt, tarragon, ground black pepper, and dried cilantro. 3. After this, top the fish with spring onions, peppercorns, and ghee. 4. Install the crisper plate in both baskets, put the salmon pockets in one layer in the baskets, and insert the baskets into the unit. Select Zone 1 and select AIR FRY. Then set the temperature to 385°F and set the time to 15 minutes. Select MATCH COOK to match the Settings in Zone 2 with those in Zone 1. Then select START/PAUSE to begin. 5. Once cooking has finished, serve.
Per Serving: Calories 171; Fat 10. 19g; Sodium 673mg; Carbs 1. 2g; Fiber 0. 3g; Sugar 0. 49g; Protein 17. 84g

Easy Shrimp with Scallions
Prep Time: 3 minutes | Cook Time: 10 minutes | Serves: 4

1 pound shrimp, peeled and deveined
2 tablespoons olive oil

1 tablespoon scallions, chopped
1 cup chicken stock

1. Install the crisper plate in the basket, put the shrimp in the basket, mixing the shrimp with the oil, onion and the stock, and onion. Insert the basket into the unit. 2. Select Zone 1 and select AIR FRY. Then set the temperature to 380°F and set the time to 10 minutes. Select START/PAUSE to begin. 3. Once cooking has finished, divide into bowls and serve.
Per Serving: Calories 178; Fat 8. 05g; Sodium 221mg; Carbs 2. 23g; Fiber 0g; Sugar 0. 98g; Protein 24. 33g

Lemony Chili Octopus
Prep Time: 10 minutes | Cook Time: 26 minutes | Serves: 4

11 oz octopus
1 teaspoon chili flakes
1 chili pepper, chopped
1 tablespoon coconut oil, melted

½ teaspoon salt
1 cup of water
1 tablespoon lemon juice

1. Pour the water in the pan and bring it to boil. Chop the octopus and put it in the boiling water. Close the lid and cook the seafood for 25 minutes. After this, remove the octopus from the water and sprinkle with the chili flakes, coconut oil, salt, chili pepper, and lemon juice. 2. Install the crisper plate in both baskets, put the octopus in the baskets, and insert the baskets into the unit. Select Zone 1 and select AIR FRY. Then set the temperature to 390°F and set the time to 1 minutes. Select MATCH COOK to match the Settings in Zone 2 with those in Zone 1. Then select START/PAUSE to begin. 3. Once cooking has finished, serve.
Per Serving: Calories 100; Fat 4. 34g; Sodium 491mg; Carbs 3. 38g; Fiber 0. 4g; Sugar 0. 72g; Protein 11. 96g

Crispy Spicy Shrimp

Prep Time: 20 minutes | Cook Time: 8 minutes | Serves: 4

Shrimp:
1 pound (26–30 count) shrimp, peeled, deveined, and butterflied (last tail section of shell intact)

Marinade:
1 5-ounce can evaporated milk
2 eggs, beaten

2 tablespoons white vinegar
1 tablespoon baking powder

Coating:
1 cup crushed panko breadcrumbs
½ teaspoon paprika
½ teaspoon Old Bay Seasoning

¼ teaspoon garlic powder
Oil for misting or cooking spray

1. Stir together all marinade ingredients until well mixed. Add the shrimp and stir to coat. Refrigerate for 1 hour. 2. Combine the coating ingredients in a shallow dish. 3. Remove the shrimp from marinade, roll in the crumb mixture, and spray with olive oil or cooking spray. 4. Install the crisper plate in both baskets, put the shrimp in the baskets, in single layer, close but not overlapping. Insert the baskets into the unit. 5. Select Zone 1 and select AIR FRY. Then set the temperature to 390°F and set the time to 8 minutes. Select MATCH COOK to match the Settings in Zone 2 with those in Zone 1. Then select START/PAUSE to begin. Cook until light golden brown and crispy. 6. Once cooking has finished, serve.

Per Serving: Calories 210; Fat 6. 85g; Sodium 318mg; Carbs 8. 82g; Fiber 1. 4g; Sugar 4. 84g; Protein 29. 47g

Lemony Shrimp & Grits

Prep Time: 15 minutes | Cook Time: 21 minutes | Serves: 4

1 pound raw shelled shrimp, deveined (26–30 count or smaller)

Marinade:
2 tablespoons lemon juice
2 tablespoons Worcestershire sauce
1 tablespoon olive oil

1 teaspoon Old Bay Seasoning
½ teaspoon hot sauce

Grits:
¾ cup quick cooking grits (not instant)
3 cups water
½ teaspoon salt
1 tablespoon butter
½ cup chopped green bell pepper

½ cup chopped celery
½ cup chopped onion
½ teaspoon oregano
¼ teaspoon Old Bay Seasoning
2 ounces sharp Cheddar cheese, grated

1. Stir together all marinade ingredients. Pour the marinade over the shrimp and set aside. 2. For the grits, heat the water and salt to boil in a saucepan on stovetop. Stir in the grits, reduce the heat to medium-low, and cook about 5 minutes or until thick and done. 3. Place the butter, celery, bell pepper, and onion in a pan. Install the crisper plate in the basket, put the mixture in the basket, and insert the basket into the unit. Select Zone 1 and select AIR FRY. Then set the temperature to 390°F and set the time to 2 minutes. Select START/PAUSE to begin. Stir and cook 6 or 7 minutes longer, until crisp tender. 4. Add the oregano and 1 teaspoon Old Bay to cooked vegetables. Stir in grits and cheese and cook at 390°F for 1 minute. Stir and cook 1 to 2 minutes longer to melt cheese. 5. Remove the basket. Cover with plate to keep warm while shrimp cooks. 6. Drain marinade from shrimp. Place the shrimp in the basket and cook at 360°F for 3 minutes. Stir or shake the basket. Cook 2 to 4 more minutes, until done. 7. When cooking is up, to serve, spoon grits onto plates and top with shrimp.

Per Serving: Calories 267; Fat 13. 28g; Sodium 745mg; Carbs 10. 3g; Fiber 1g; Sugar 2. 2g; Protein 27. 17g

Golden Coconut Sardines
Prep Time: 15 minutes | Cook Time: 10 minutes | Serves: 5

12 oz sardines, trimmed, cleaned
1 cup coconut flour

1 tablespoon coconut oil
1 teaspoon salt

1. Sprinkle the sardines with salt and coat in the coconut flour. 2. Then grease the crisper plate with coconut oil. 3. Install the crisper plate in both baskets, place the sardines in the baskets, and insert the baskets into the unit. Select Zone 1 and select AIR FRY. Then set the temperature to 385°F and set the time to 10 minutes. Select MATCH COOK to match the Settings in Zone 2 with those in Zone 1. Select START/PAUSE to begin. 4. Once cooking has finished, serve.
Per Serving: Calories 174; Fat 10. 61g; Sodium 724mg; Carbs 1. 78g; Fiber 0. 5g; Sugar 1. 25g; Protein 17. 1g

Bacon Wrapped Halibut
Prep Time: 15 minutes | Cook Time: 10 minutes | Serves: 4

24 oz halibut steaks (6 oz each fillet)
1 teaspoon avocado oil

1 teaspoon ground black pepper
4 oz bacon, sliced

1. Sprinkle the halibut steaks with avocado oil and ground black pepper. 2. Then wrap the fish in the bacon slices. 3. Install the crisper plate in both baskets, place the fish in the baskets, and insert the baskets into the unit. Select Zone 1 and select AIR FRY. Then set the temperature to 390°F and set the time to 10 minutes. Select MATCH COOK to match the Settings in Zone 2 with those in Zone 1. Select START/PAUSE to begin. Cook the fish for 5 minutes per side. 4. Once cooking has finished, serve.
Per Serving: Calories 416; Fat 33. 06g; Sodium 552mg; Carbs 2. 26g; Fiber 0. 9g; Sugar 0g; Protein 27. 55g

Bell Pepper–Stuffed Mackerel
Prep Time: 15 minutes | Cook Time: 20 minutes | Serves: 5

1-pound mackerel, trimmed
1 bell pepper, chopped
½ cup spinach, chopped

1 tablespoon avocado oil
1 teaspoon ground black pepper
1 teaspoon keto tomato paste

1. In the mixing bowl, mix bell pepper with ground black pepper, spinach, and tomato paste. 2. Fill the mackerel with spinach mixture. Then brush the fish with avocado oil. 3. Install the crisper plate in the basket, place the fish in the basket, and insert the basket into the unit. Select Zone 1 and select AIR FRY. Then set the temperature to 365°F and set the time to 20 minutes. Select START/PAUSE to begin. 4. Once cooking has finished, serve.
Per Serving: Calories 127; Fat 4. 67g; Sodium 147mg; Carbs 1. 54g; Fiber 0. 4g; Sugar 0. 61g; Protein 18. 77g

Cheesy Coconut Shrimp

Prep Time: 15 minutes | Cook Time: 5 minutes | Serves: 4

14 oz shrimps, peeled
1 egg, beaten
½ cup of coconut milk

1 cup Cheddar cheese, shredded
½ teaspoon coconut oil
1 teaspoon ground coriander

1. In the mixing bowl, mix shrimps with egg, Cheddar cheese, coconut milk, coconut oil, and ground coriander. 2. Install the crisper plate in both baskets, place the mixture in the baskets, and insert the baskets into the unit. Select Zone 1 and select AIR FRY. Then set the temperature to 400°F and set the time to 5 minutes. Select MATCH COOK to match the Settings in Zone 2 with those in Zone 1. Select START/PAUSE to begin. 3. Once cooking has finished, serve.

Per Serving: Calories 308; Fat 20. 44g; Sodium 351mg; Carbs 2. 18g; Fiber 0. 7g; Sugar 1. 14g; Protein 29. 95g

Turmeric Chili Cod

Prep Time: 10 minutes | Cook Time: 7 minutes | Serves: 2

12 oz cod fillet
1 teaspoon ground turmeric
1 teaspoon chili flakes

1 tablespoon coconut oil, melted
½ teaspoon salt

1. Mix coconut oil with chili flakes, ground turmeric, and salt. 2. Then mix cod fillet with ground turmeric. 3. Install the crisper plate in the basket, place the cod fillet in the basket, and insert the basket into the unit. Select Zone 1 and select AIR FRY. Then set the temperature to 385°F and set the time to 7 minutes. Select START/PAUSE to begin. 4. Once cooking has finished, serve.

Per Serving: Calories 560; Fat 37. 66g; Sodium 1454mg; Carbs 16. 99g; Fiber 11. 2g; Sugar 1. 51g; Protein 39. 45g

Provolone Salmon Fillet

Prep Time: 5 minutes | Cook Time: 15 minutes | Serves: 4

1-pound salmon fillet, chopped
2 oz Provolone, grated

1 teaspoon avocado oil
¼ teaspoon ground paprika

1. Sprinkle the salmon fillets with avocado oil. 2. Install the crisper plate in the basket, place the fish in the basket, sprinkle the fish with ground paprika and top with Provolone cheese. Insert the basket into the unit. 3. Select Zone 1 and select AIR FRY. Then set the temperature to 360°F and set the time to 15 minutes. Select START/PAUSE to begin. 4. Once cooking has finished, serve.

Per Serving: Calories 234; Fat 13. 05g; Sodium 615mg; Carbs 0. 38g; Fiber 0. 1g; Sugar 0. 09g; Protein 27. 04g

Mustard Tuna Steak

Prep Time: 10 minutes | Cook Time: 12 minutes | Serves: 4

1-pound tuna steaks, boneless and cubed
1 tablespoon mustard

1 tablespoon avocado oil
1 tablespoon apple cider vinegar

1. Mix avocado oil with mustard and apple cider vinegar. 2. Then brush tuna steaks with mustard mixture. 3. Install the crisper plate in the basket, place the tuna steaks in the basket, and insert the basket into the unit. Select Zone 1 and select AIR FRY. Then set the temperature to 360°F and set the time to 12 minutes. Select START/PAUSE to begin. 4. Cook the fish for 6 minutes per side. 5. Once cooking has finished, serve.
Per Serving: Calories 132; Fat 4. 72g; Sodium 323mg; Carbs 0. 26g; Fiber 0. 2g; Sugar 0. 05g; Protein 22. 19g

Cumin Mussels

Prep Time: 10 minutes | Cook Time: 2 minutes | Serves: 5

2-pounds mussels, cleaned, peeled
1 teaspoon onion powder
1 teaspoon ground cumin

1 tablespoon avocado oil
¼ cup apple cider vinegar

1. Mix mussels with onion powder, avocado oil, ground cumin, and apple cider vinegar. 2. Install the crisper plate in both baskets, place the mussels in the baskets, and insert the baskets into the unit. Select Zone 1 and select AIR FRY. Then set the temperature to 390°F and set the time to 2 minutes. Select MATCH COOK to match the Settings in Zone 2 with those in Zone 1. Select START/PAUSE to begin. 3. Once cooking has finished, serve.
Per Serving: Calories 190; Fat 6. 98g; Sodium 520mg; Carbs 8. 66g; Fiber 0. 1g; Sugar 1. 23g; Protein 21. 73g

Lemony Tomatillos Cod

Prep Time: 10 minutes | Cook Time: 15 minutes | Serves: 4

2 oz tomatillos, chopped
1-pound cod fillet, roughly chopped

1 tablespoon avocado oil
1 tablespoon lemon juice

1. Mix avocado oil with lemon juice and tomato paste. 2. Then mix cod fillet with tomato mixture. 3. Install the crisper plate in the basket, place the cod fillet in the basket, and add lemon juice and tomatillos. Insert the basket into the unit. 4. Select Zone 1 and select AIR FRY. Then set the temperature to 375°F and set the time to 15 minutes. Select START/PAUSE to begin. 5. Once cooking has finished, serve.
Per Serving: Calories 115; Fat 4. 12g; Sodium 344mg; Carbs 1. 09g; Fiber 0. 3g; Sugar 0. 65g; Protein 17. 47g

Coconut Cream Salmon with Endives

Prep Time: 5 minutes | Cook Time: 20 minutes | Serves: 4

2 endives, shredded
1-pound salmon fillet, chopped
1 tablespoon ghee

1 teaspoon ground coriander
¼ cup coconut cream

1. Install the crisper plate in the basket, place all ingredients in the basket, shaking gently, and insert the basket into the unit. 2. Select Zone 1 and select AIR FRY. Then set the temperature to 360°F and set the time to 20 minutes. Select START/PAUSE to begin. Shake the fish every 5 minutes. 3. Once cooking has finished, serve.
Per Serving: Calories 297; Fat 17. 25g; Sodium 548mg; Carbs 9. 59g; Fiber 8. 3g; Sugar 0. 64g; Protein 27. 15g

Chapter 6 Snacks and Appetizers

Paprika Pumpkin Seeds

Prep Time: 10 minutes | Cook Time: 45 minutes | Serves: 3

1½ cups pumpkin seeds from a large whole pumpkin
Olive oil

1½ tsp. salt
1 tsp. smoked paprika

1. Boil two quarts of well-salted water in a pot. Cook the pumpkin seeds in the boiling water for 10 minutes. 2. Dump the content of the pot into a sieve and dry the seeds on paper towels for at least 20 minutes. 3. Cover the seeds with salt, olive oil, and smoked paprika. 4. Install the crisper plate in the basket, place the seeds in the basket, and insert the basket into the unit. 5. Select Zone 1 and select AIR FRY. Then set the temperature to 350°F and set the time to 35 minutes. Select START/PAUSE to begin. Give the basket a good shake several times throughout the cooking process until crispy and lightly browned. 6. Once cooking has finished, let the seeds cool before serving. Alternatively, you can keep them in an air-tight container or bag for snacking or for use as a yogurt topping.
Per Serving: Calories 350; Fat 30. 04g; Sodium 1314mg; Carbs 9. 09g; Fiber 4. 1g; Sugar 0. 84g; Protein 17. 71g

Cocktail Flanks Rolls

Prep Time: 10 minutes | Cook Time: 11 minutes | Serves: 4

1x 12-oz. package cocktail franks

1x 8-oz. can crescent rolls

1. Drain the cocktail franks and dry with paper towels. 2. Unroll the crescent rolls and slice the dough into rectangular strips, roughly 1" by 1. 5". 3. Wrap the franks in the strips with the ends poking out. Place in the freezer for 5 minutes. 4. Take the franks out of the freezer. 5. Install the crisper plate in both baskets, place the franks in the baskets, and insert the baskets into the unit. Select Zone 1 and select AIR FRY. Then set the temperature to 330°F and set the time to 8 minutes. Select MATCH COOK to match the Settings in Zone 2 with those in Zone 1. Select START/PAUSE to begin. 6. Turn the temperature to 390°F and cook for another 3 minutes until a golden-brown color is achieved. 7. Once cooking has finished, serve.
Per Serving: Calories 402; Fat 2. 14g; Sodium 284mg; Carbs 89. 33g; Fiber 1. 2g; Sugar 24. 47g; Protein 5. 66g

Garlic Mushroom Cups

Prep Time: 10 minutes | Cook Time: 8 minutes | Serves: 4

16 small button mushrooms
For the Stuffing:
1½ slices bread
1 garlic clove, crushed
1 tbsp. flat-leafed parsley, finely chopped

Ground black pepper to taste
1½ tbsp. olive oil

1. Blend together the bread slices, parsley, pepper, and garlic until a fine crumb is formed. 2. Mix in the olive oil. 3. Remove the mushroom stalks and spoon even amounts of the filling into the caps. Press the crumbs in well to make sure none fall out. 4. Install the crisper plate in both baskets, place the mushroom caps in the baskets, and insert the baskets into the unit. 5. Select Zone 1 and select AIR FRY. Then set the temperature to 390°F and set the time to 8 minutes. Select MATCH COOK to match the Settings in Zone 2 with those in Zone 1. Select START/PAUSE to begin. 6. Cook the cups for 7 to 8 minutes or until they turn golden and crispy. 7. Once cooking has finished, serve.
Per Serving: Calories 77; Fat 5. 49g; Sodium 40mg; Carbs 5. 69g; Fiber 0. 8g; Sugar 1. 24g; Protein 2. 04g

Dill Eggplant Chips
Prep Time: 10 minutes | Cook Time: 13 minutes | Serves: 4

2 eggplants, peeled and thinly sliced
Salt
½ cup tapioca starch
¼ cup canola oil

½ cup water
1 tsp. garlic powder
½ tsp. dried dill weed
½ tsp. ground black pepper, to taste

1. Season the eggplant slices with salt and leave for half an hour. 2. Run them under cold water to rinse off any excess salt. 3. In a bowl, coat the eggplant slices with all of the other ingredients. 4. Install the crisper plate in both baskets, place the eggplant slices in the baskets, and insert the baskets into the unit. Select Zone 1 and select AIR FRY. Then set the temperature to 390°F and set the time to 13 minutes. Select MATCH COOK to match the Settings in Zone 2 with those in Zone 1. Select START/PAUSE to begin. 5. Once cooking has finished, serve with the dipping sauce of your choice.
Per Serving: Calories 262; Fat 14. 14g; Sodium 589mg; Carbs 34. 13g; Fiber 8. 6g; Sugar 10. 61g; Protein 2. 99g

Lemony Sage Potatoes
Prep Time: 10 minutes | Cook Time: 15 minutes | Serves: 8

1½ lb. fingerling potatoes, halved lengthwise
2 tbsp. melted butter
¼ cup fresh sage leaves, finely chopped
2 sprigs thyme, chopped

1 tsp. lemon zest, finely grated
¼ tsp. ground pepper
1 tbsp. sea salt flakes
½ tsp. grated ginger

1. Place the potatoes in a bowl of cold water and allow to absorb for about half an hour. 2. Dry them with a clean kitchen towel. Mix potatoes with other ingredients and toss well. 3. Install the crisper plate in the basket, place the potatoes in the basket, and insert the basket into the unit. Select Zone 1, select ROAST. Then set the temperature to 400°F and set the time to 15 minutes. Select START/PAUSE to begin. 4. Once cooking has finished, serve with tomato ketchup and mayonnaise if desired.
Per Serving: Calories 95; Fat 3. 09g; Sodium 900mg; Carbs 15. 72g; Fiber 2. 3g; Sugar 0. 77g; Protein 1. 9g

Dijon & Quinoa Tomato Meatballs
Prep Time: 10 minutes | Cook Time: 15 minutes | Serves: 6

½ lb. ground pork
½ lb. ground beef
1 cup quinoa, cooked
1 egg, beaten
2 scallions, finely chopped
½ tsp. onion powder
1½ tbsp. Dijon mustard

¾ cup ketchup
1 tsp. ancho chili powder
1 tbsp. sesame oil
2 tbsp. tamari sauce
¼ cup balsamic vinegar
2 tbsp. sugar

1. In a bowl, stir together all the ingredients and combine well. 2. Shape equal amounts of the mixture into small meatballs with hands. 3. Install the crisper plate in the basket, place the meatballs in the basket, and insert the basket into the unit. Select Zone 1 and select AIR FRY. Then set the temperature to 370°F and set the time to 10 minutes. Select START/PAUSE to begin. Give the basket a good shake and allow to cook for another 5 minutes. 4. Once cooking has finished, serve.
Per Serving: Calories 376; Fat 18. 66g; Sodium 439mg; Carbs 32. 42g; Fiber 2. 7g; Sugar 11. 12g; Protein 19. 99g

Ricotta Balls with Chives
Prep Time: 10 minutes | Cook Time: 8 minutes | Serves: 2-4

2 cups ricotta, grated
2 eggs, separated
2 tbsp. chives, finely chopped
2 tbsp. fresh basil, finely chopped
For coating:
¼ cup friendly bread crumbs

4 tbsp. flour
¼ tsp. salt to taste
¼ tsp. pepper powder to taste
1 tsp. orange zest, grated

1 tbsp. vegetable oil

1. In a bowl, combine the yolks, chives, salt, flour, pepper, and orange zest. 2. Throw in the ricotta and incorporate with hands. 3. Mold equal amounts of the mixture into balls. 4. Mix the oil with the bread crumbs until a crumbly consistency is achieved. 5. Coat the balls in the bread crumbs. Install the crisper plate in the basket, place the balls in the basket, and insert the basket into the unit. 5. Select Zone 1 and select AIR FRY. Then set the temperature to 390°F and set the time to 8 minutes. Select START/PAUSE to begin. Cook until a golden brown. 6. Once cooking has finished, serve with a sauce of your choosing, such as ketchup.
Per Serving: Calories 347; Fat 24. 49g; Sodium 312mg; Carbs 11. 83g; Fiber 0. 4g; Sugar 1. 09g; Protein 19. 6g

Spiced Mixed Nuts
Prep Time: 10 minutes | Cook Time: 25 minutes | Serves: 3

1 egg white, lightly beaten
¼ cup sugar
1 tsp. salt
½ tsp. ground cinnamon
¼ tsp. ground cloves

¼ tsp. ground allspice
Pinch ground cayenne pepper
1 cup pecan halves
1 cup cashews

1. Combine the egg white with the sugar and spices in a bowl. 2. Coat the crisper plate with vegetable oil. 3. Cover the nuts with the spiced egg white. Install the crisper plate in both baskets, place the nuts in the baskets, and insert the baskets into the unit. 4. Select Zone 1 and select AIR FRY. Then set the temperature to 300°F and set the time to 25 minutes. Select MATCH COOK to match the Settings in Zone 2 with those in Zone 1. Select START/PAUSE to begin. Give the nuts a few good stirs throughout the cooking time until they are crunchy and toasted. 5. Once cooking has finished, serve immediately. Or place in an airtight container and store for up to two weeks.
Per Serving: Calories 431; Fat 36. 28g; Sodium 799mg; Carbs 23. 53g; Fiber 4. 7g; Sugar 11. 99g; Protein 9. 73g

Spiced Shrimp with Bacon
Prep Time: 10 minutes | Cook Time: 8 minutes | Serves: 10

1¼ lb. shrimp, peeled and deveined
1 tsp. paprika
½ tsp. ground black pepper
½ tsp. red pepper flakes, crushed
1 tbsp. salt

1 tsp. chili powder
1 tbsp. shallot powder
¼ tsp. cumin powder
1¼ lb. thin bacon slices

1. Coat the shrimps with all of the seasonings. 2. Wrap a slice of bacon around each shrimp, and hold it in place with a toothpick. Refrigerate for half an hour. 3. Install the crisper plate in both baskets, place the shrimp in the baskets, and insert the baskets into the unit. Select Zone 1 and select AIR FRY. Then set the temperature to 360°F and set the time to 8 minutes. Select MATCH COOK to match the Settings in Zone 2 with those in Zone 1. Select START/PAUSE to begin. 4. Once cooking has finished, serve.
Per Serving: Calories 135; Fat 2. 9g; Sodium 1630mg; Carbs 0. 87g; Fiber 0. 3g; Sugar 0. 35g; Protein 25. 58g

Delicious Roasted Parsnip

Prep Time: 10 minutes | Cook Time: 42 minutes | Serves: 5

2 lb. parsnips [about 6 large parsnips]
2 tbsp. maple syrup

1 tbsp. coconut oil
1 tbsp. parsley, dried flakes

1. Install the crisper plate in both baskets, put the olive oil and Maggi sauce in the baskets, and insert the baskets into the unit. Select Zone 1 and select AIR FRY. Then set the temperature to 320°F and set the time to 2 minutes. Select MATCH COOK to match the Settings in Zone 2 with those in Zone 1. Then select START/PAUSE to begin. Melt the duck fat or coconut oil in the basket for 2 minutes. 2. Rinse the parsnips to clean them and dry them. Chop into 1-inch cubes. Transfer to the basket. 3. Cook the parsnip cubes in the fat/oil for 35 minutes, tossing them regularly. 4. Season the parsnips with parsley and maple syrup and allow to cook for another 5 minutes or longer to achieve a soft texture throughout. 5. Once cooking has finished, serve straightaway.

Per Serving: Calories 173; Fat 3. 28g; Sodium 20mg; Carbs 36. 27g; Fiber 6. 6g; Sugar 13. 55g; Protein 2. 42g

Cheesy Chicken Zucchini Boats

Prep Time: 15 minutes | Cook Time: 10 minutes | Serves: 2

1 cup ground chicken
1 zucchini
1½ cups crushed tomatoes
½ tsp. salt
¼ tsp. pepper

½ tsp. garlic powder
2 tbsp. butter or olive oil
½ cup cheese, grated
¼ tsp. dried oregano

1. Peel and halve the zucchini. Use a spoon to scoop out the flesh. 2. In a bowl, combine the ground chicken, tomato, butter, cheese, oregano, salt, garlic powder, and pepper. Fill in the hollowed-out zucchini with this mixture. 3. Install the crisper plate in both baskets, put the mixture in the baskets, and insert the baskets into the unit. Select Zone 1 and select BAKE. Then set the temperature to 400°F and set the time to 10 minutes. Select MATCH COOK to match the Settings in Zone 2 with those in Zone 1. Then select START/PAUSE to begin. 4. Once cooking has finished, serve warm.

Per Serving: Calories 491; Fat 25. 37g; Sodium 900mg; Carbs 5. 97g; Fiber 1. 6g; Sugar 3. 43g; Protein 58. 43g

Yummy Coconut Cheese Sticks

Prep Time: 10 minutes | Cook Time: 4 minutes | Serves: 4

1 egg, beaten
4 tablespoons coconut flakes
1 teaspoon ground paprika

6 óz Provolone cheese
Cooking spray

1. Cut the cheese into sticks. Then dip every cheese stick in the beaten egg. 2. After this, mix up coconut flakes and ground paprika. Coat the cheese sticks in the coconut mixture. 3. Install the crisper plate in the basket, put the cheese sticks in the basket and spray them with cooking spray. Insert the basket into the unit. Select Zone 1 and select AIR FRY. Then set the temperature to 400°F and set the time 2 minutes. Select START/PAUSE to begin. Cook the meal for 2 minutes from each side. 4. Once cooking has finished, cool them well before serving.

Per Serving: Calories 197; Fat 14. 67g; Sodium 404mg; Carbs 4. 05g; Fiber 0. 7g; Sugar 2. 29g; Protein 12. 51g

Cheesy Garlic Broccoli Bites
Prep Time: 10 minutes | Cook Time: 15 minutes | Serves: 4

1 pound broccoli florets
1 teaspoon granulated garlic
1 tablespoon onion flakes, dried

1 teaspoon red pepper flakes, crushed
2 tablespoons olive oil
½ cup Pecorino Romano cheese, grated

1. Spray the crisper plate with olive oil. 2. Install the crisper plate in the basket, place all ingredients in the basket, and insert the basket into the unit. 3. Select Zone 1 and select AIR FRY. Then set the temperature to 370°F and set the time to 10 minutes. Select START/PAUSE to begin. 4. Shake the basket halfway through the cooking time. 5. Once cooking has finished, serve. Enjoy!

Per Serving: Calories 143; Fat 10. 8g; Sodium 263mg; Carbs 6. 29g; Fiber 3. 2g; Sugar 0. 95g; Protein 7. 31g

Juicy Chocolate Bacon Bites
Prep Time: 5 minutes | Cook Time: 10 minutes | Serves: 4

4 bacon slices, halved
1 cup dark chocolate, melted

A pinch of pink salt

1. Dip each bacon slice in some chocolate and sprinkle pink salt over them. 2. Install the crisper plate in the basket, put the bacon slices in the basket, and insert the basket into the unit. Select Zone 1 and select AIR FRY. Then set the temperature to 350°F and set the time to 10 minutes. Select START/PAUSE to begin. 3. Once cooking has finished, serve as a snack.

Per Serving: Calories 162; Fat 12. 36g; Sodium 742mg; Carbs 8. 14g; Fiber 0. 3g; Sugar 0. 22g; Protein 5. 41g

Coconut Shrimp Balls
Prep Time: 5 minutes | Cook Time: 15 minutes | Serves: 4

1 pound shrimp, peeled, deveined and minced
1 egg, whisked
3 tablespoons coconut, shredded

½ cup coconut flour
1 tablespoon avocado oil
1 tablespoon cilantro, chopped

1. In a bowl, mix all the ingredients, stir well and shape medium balls out of this mix. 2. Install the crisper plate in both baskets, put the balls in the lined baskets, and insert the baskets into the unit. Select Zone 1 and select AIR FRY. Then set the temperature to 350°F and set the time to 15 minutes. Select MATCH COOK to match the Settings in Zone 2 with those in Zone 1. Then select START/PAUSE to begin. 3. Once cooking has finished, serve as an appetizer.

Per Serving: Calories 151; Fat 5. 24g; Sodium 194mg; Carbs 1. 62g; Fiber 0. 5g; Sugar 1. 12g; Protein 24. 48g

Cheesy Butter Brussels Sprouts
Prep Time: 10 minutes | Cook Time: 10 minutes | Serves: 4

1 pound Brussels sprouts, trimmed
2 tablespoons butter, melted
Sea salt and freshly ground black pepper, to taste

1 teaspoon garlic, minced
2 tablespoons red wine vinegar
2 ounces cheddar cheese, shredded

1. Toss the Brussels sprouts with the remaining ingredients. 2. Install the crisper plate in the basket, place the Brussels sprouts in the basket, and insert the basket into the unit. 3. Select Zone 1 and select AIR FRY. Then set the temperature to 380°F and set the time to 10 minutes. Select START/PAUSE to begin. 4. Shake the basket halfway through the cooking time. 5. Once cooking has finished, serve warm and enjoy!

Per Serving: Calories 129; Fat 7. 38g; Sodium 812mg; Carbs 12. 29g; Fiber 4. 5g; Sugar 3. 51g; Protein 5. 9g

Crunchy Almond Coconut Granola
Prep Time: 10 minutes | Cook Time: 12 minutes | Serves: 4

1 teaspoon monk fruit
1 teaspoon almond butter
1 teaspoon coconut oil
2 tablespoons almonds, chopped
1 teaspoon pumpkin puree
½ teaspoon pumpkin pie spices

2 tablespoons coconut flakes
2 tablespoons pumpkin seeds, crushed
1 teaspoon hemp seeds
1 teaspoon flax seeds
Cooking spray

1. In the big bowl, mix up the almond butter and coconut oil. Microwave the mixture until it is melted. 2. After this, in the separated bowl, mix up the monk fruit, pumpkin spices, hemp seeds, coconut flakes, pumpkin seeds, and flax seeds. Add the melted coconut oil and pumpkin puree. 3. Then stir the mixture until it is homogenous. 4. Then put the pumpkin mixture on the baking paper and make the shape of the square. 5. After this, cut the square on the serving bars. Install the crisper plate in the basket, put the bars in the basket, and insert the basket into the unit. Select Zone 1 and select AIR FRY. Then set the temperature to 350°F and set the time to 12 minutes. Select START/PAUSE to begin. Cook the pumpkin granola for 12 minutes. 6. Once cooking has finished, serve.
Per Serving: Calories 75; Fat 6. 77g; Sodium 27mg; Carbs 2. 83g; Fiber 0. 8g; Sugar 1. 34g; Protein 1. 83g

Pickled Dill Bacon Bowls
Prep Time: 5 minutes | Cook Time: 20 minutes | Serves: 4

4 dill pickle spears, sliced in half and quartered
8 bacon slices, halved

1 cup avocado mayonnaise

1. Wrap each pickle spear in a bacon slice. 2. Install the crisper plate in both baskets, put the dill pickle spears in the baskets, and insert the baskets into the unit. Select Zone 1 and select AIR FRY. Then set the temperature to 400°F and set the time to 20 minutes. Select MATCH COOK to match the Settings in Zone 2 with those in Zone 1. Then select START/PAUSE to begin. 3. Once cooking has finished, divide into bowls and serve as a snack with the mayonnaise.
Per Serving: Calories 124; Fat 7. 09g; Sodium 483mg; Carbs 4. 1g; Fiber 2. 6g; Sugar 0. 84g; Protein 12. 32g

Tomato Bacon Smokies
Prep Time: 15 minutes | Cook Time: 10 minutes | Serves: 10

12 oz pork and beef smokies
3 oz bacon, sliced
1 teaspoon keto tomato sauce

1 teaspoon Erythritol
1 teaspoon avocado oil
½ teaspoon cayenne pepper

1. Sprinkle the smokies with cayenne pepper and tomato sauce. Then sprinkle them with Erythritol and olive oil. 2. After this, wrap every smokie in the bacon and secure it with the toothpick. 3. Install the crisper plate in both baskets, put the bacon smokies in the baskets, and insert the baskets into the unit. Select Zone 1 and select AIR FRY. Then set the temperature to 400°F and set the time to 10 minutes. Select MATCH COOK to match the Settings in Zone 2 with those in Zone 1. Then select START/PAUSE to begin. 4. Shake them gently during cooking to avoid burning. 5. Once cooking has finished, serve.
Per Serving: Calories 166; Fat 15. 34g; Sodium 448mg; Carbs 1. 62g; Fiber 0. 3g; Sugar 0. 07g; Protein 5. 63g

Spicy Avocado Balls

Prep Time: 5 minutes | Cook Time: 5 minutes | Serves: 4

1 avocado, peeled, pitted and mashed
¼ cup ghee, melted
2 garlic cloves, minced
2 spring onions, minced
1 chili pepper, chopped

1 tablespoon lime juice
2 tablespoons cilantro
A pinch of salt and black pepper
4 bacon slices, cooked and crumbled
Cooking spray

1. Mix all the ingredients except the cooking spray in a bowl, stir well and shape medium balls out of this mix. 2. Install the crisper plate in the basket, put the ingredients in the basket and grease with cooking spray. Insert the basket into the unit. Select Zone 1 and select AIR FRY. Then set the temperature to 370°F and set the time to 5 minutes. Select START/PAUSE to begin. 3. Once cooking has finished, serve as a snack.
Per Serving: Calories 321; Fat 31. 27g; Sodium 129mg; Carbs 8. 01g; Fiber 4g; Sugar 1. 95g; Protein 4. 97g

Easy Pork Rinds

Prep Time: 10 minutes | Cook Time: 10 minutes | Serves: 3

6 oz pork skin
1 tablespoon keto tomato sauce

1 teaspoon olive oil

1. Chop the pork skin into the rinds and sprinkle with the sauce and olive oil. Mix up well. 2. Install the crisper plate in the basket, put the pork skin rinds in the basket in one layer, and insert the basket into the unit. Select Zone 1 and select AIR FRY. Then set the temperature to 400°F and set the time to 10 minutes. Select START/PAUSE to begin. 3. Flip the rinds on another side after 5 minutes of cooking. 4. Once cooking has finished, serve.
Per Serving: Calories 135; Fat 6. 87g; Sodium 110mg; Carbs 1. 13g; Fiber 0. 3g; Sugar 0. 6g; Protein 15. 89g

Crispy Cheese Zucchini Chips

Prep Time: 10 minutes | Cook Time: 13 minutes | Serves: 8

2 zucchinis, thinly sliced
4 tablespoons almond flour
2 oz Parmesan

2 eggs, beaten
½ teaspoon white pepper
Cooking spray

1. In the big bowl, mix up almond flour, Parmesan, and white pepper. Then dip the zucchini slices in the egg and coat in the almond flour mixture. 2. Install the crisper plate in both baskets, put the prepared zucchini slices in the baskets in one layer, and insert the baskets into the unit. Select Zone 1 and select AIR FRY. Then set the temperature to 355°F and set the time to 10 minutes. Select MATCH COOK to match the Settings in Zone 2 with those in Zone 1. Then select START/PAUSE to begin. 3. Then flip the vegetables on another side and cook them for 3 minutes more or until crispy. 4. Once cooking has finished, serve.
Per Serving: Calories 50; Fat 2. 09g; Sodium 97mg; Carbs 3. 23g; Fiber 0. 1g; Sugar 0. 17g; Protein 4. 43g

Cajun Spicy Snack

Prep Time: 10 minutes | Cook Time: 10 minutes | Serves: 5

2 tbsp. Cajun or Creole seasoning
½ cup butter, melted
2 cups peanut
2 cups mini wheat thin crackers
2 cups mini pretzels
2 tsp. salt
1 tsp. cayenne pepper

4 cups plain popcorn
1 tsp. paprika
1 tsp. garlic
½ tsp. thyme
½ tsp. oregano
1 tsp. black pepper
½ tsp. onion powder

1. In a bowl, combine the Cajun spice with the melted butter. 2. Stir together the peanuts, popcorn, crackers, and pretzels in a separate bowl. Coat the snacks with the butter mixture. 3. Install the crisper plate in both baskets, place the snacks in the baskets, and insert the baskets into the unit. Select Zone 1 and select AIR FRY. Then set the temperature to 370°F and set the time to 10 minutes. Select MATCH COOK to match the Settings in Zone 2 with those in Zone 1. Select START/PAUSE to begin. 4. Shake the basket frequently during the cooking time. 5. Once cooking has finished, put the snack mix on a cookie sheet and leave to cool. The snacks can be kept in an airtight container for up to one week.

Per Serving: Calories 744; Fat 50. 61g; Sodium 1459mg; Carbs 59. 01g; Fiber 12g; Sugar 3. 71g; Protein 23. 58g

Cheesy Broccoli & Egg Balls

Prep Time: 10 minutes | Cook Time: 20 minutes | Serves: 6

2 eggs, well whisked
2 cups Colby cheese, shredded
1 cup flour
Seasoned salt, to taste

¼ tsp. ground black pepper, or more if preferred
1 head broccoli, chopped into florets
1 cup crushed saltines

1. Mix together the eggs, cheese, salt, flour, pepper, and broccoli until a dough-like paste is formed. Refrigerate for 1 hour. 2. Divide the mixture evenly and mold each portion into small balls. Coat the balls in the crushed saltines and spritz them all over with cooking spray. 3. Install the crisper plate in the basket, place the balls in the basket, and insert the basket into the unit. Select Zone 1 and select AIR FRY. Then set the temperature to 360°F and set the time to 10 minutes. Select START/PAUSE to begin. At this point, you should check how far along in the cooking process they are and allow to cook for a further 8 to 10 minutes as needed. 4. Once cooking has finished, serve with the dipping sauce of your choice.

Per Serving: Calories 343; Fat 18. 59g; Sodium 800mg; Carbs 26. 37g; Fiber 1. 1g; Sugar 0. 77g; Protein 16. 95g

Cheesy Mushrooms with Chives

Prep Time: 10 minutes | Cook Time: 7 minutes | Serves: 4

1 tablespoon butter
6 ounces Pecorino Romano cheese, grated
2 tablespoons chives, chopped
1 tablespoon minced garlic

½ teaspoon cayenne pepper
Sea salt and ground black pepper, to taste
1 pound button mushrooms, stems removed

1. Thoroughly combine the butter, chives, cheese, garlic, cayenne pepper, salt, and black pepper in a mixing bowl. 2. Divide the filling between the mushrooms. 3. Install the crisper plate in the basket, place the mushrooms in the basket, and insert the basket into the unit. Select Zone 1 and select AIR FRY. Then set the temperature to 400°F and set the time to 7 minutes. Select START/PAUSE to begin. Shake the basket halfway while cooking. 4. Once cooking has finished, serve. Bon appétit!

Per Serving: Calories 224; Fat 14. 8g; Sodium 639mg; Carbs 7. 2g; Fiber 1. 4g; Sugar 3. 2g; Protein 17. 49g

Cheesy Green Bean Fries

Prep Time: 10 minutes | Cook Time: 6 minutes | Serves: 4

1 pound green beans
4 tablespoons all-purpose flour
2 eggs, whisked
½ cup breadcrumbs
½ cup grated parmesan cheese

1 teaspoon cayenne pepper
½ teaspoon mustard seeds
1 teaspoon garlic powder
Sea salt and ground black pepper, to taste

1. In a shallow bowl, thoroughly combine the flour and eggs and mix to combine well. 2. Then, in another bowl, mix the remaining ingredients. 3. Dip the beans in the egg mixture, then in the breadcrumb mixture. 4. Install the crisper plate in the basket, place the green beans in the basket, and insert the basket into the unit. Select Zone 1 and select AIR FRY. Then set the temperature to 390°F and set the time to 6 minutes. Select START/PAUSE to begin. Toss the basket halfway through the cooking time. 5. Once cooking has finished, serve. Enjoy!
Per Serving: Calories 234; Fat 9. 81g; Sodium 379mg; Carbs 24. 77g; Fiber 3. 4g; Sugar 2. 73g; Protein 12. 39g

Hot–Spicy Chicken Drumettes

Prep Time: 10 minutes | Cook Time: 18 minutes | Serves: 4

2 pounds chicken drumettes
1 teaspoon ancho chile pepper
1 teaspoon smoked paprika
1 teaspoon onion powder

1 teaspoon garlic powder
Kosher salt and ground black pepper, to taste
¼ tsp black pepper
2 tablespoons olive oil

1. Toss the chicken drumettes with the remaining ingredients. 2. Install the crisper plate in both baskets, place the chicken drumettes in the baskets, and insert the baskets into the unit. Select Zone 1 and select AIR FRY. Then set the temperature to 380°F and set the time to 18 minutes. Select MATCH COOK to match the Settings in Zone 2 with those in Zone 1. Select START/PAUSE to begin. 3. Turn them over halfway through the cooking time. 4. Once cooking has finished, serve. Bon appétit!
Per Serving: Calories 335; Fat 13. 34g; Sodium 174mg; Carbs 4. 71g; Fiber 1. 5g; Sugar 0. 69g; Protein 47. 13g

Crispy Cheesy Cauliflower

Prep Time: 10 minutes | Cook Time: 15 minutes | Serves: 4

½ cup milk
1 cup all-purpose flour
1 teaspoon garlic powder
1 teaspoon onion powder
1 teaspoon hot paprika

Sea salt and ground black pepper, to taste
2 tablespoons olive oil
1 pound cauliflower florets
4 ounces parmesan cheese, preferably freshly grated

1. In a mixing bowl, thoroughly combine the flour, spices, milk, and olive oil. 2. Dip the cauliflower florets in the flour mixture. 3. Install the crisper plate in the basket, place the cauliflower florets in the basket, and insert the basket into the unit. Select Zone 1 and select AIR FRY. Then set the temperature to 350°F and set the time to 10 minutes. Select START/PAUSE to begin. Turn them over halfway through the cooking time. 4. Top the cauliflower florets with cheese and continue to cook another 5 minutes. 5. Once cooking has finished, serve. Bon appétit!
Per Serving: Calories 350; Fat 16. 37g; Sodium 561mg; Carbs 37. 3g; Fiber 3. 6g; Sugar 4. 5g; Protein 14. 92g

Simple Sprouts Wraps

Prep Time: 5 minutes | Cook Time: 20 minutes | Serves: 12

12 bacon strips
12 Brussels sprouts

A drizzle of olive oil

1. Wrap each Brussels sprouts in a bacon strip and brush them with some oil. 2. Install the crisper plate in both baskets, put the brussels sprouts in the baskets, and insert the baskets into the unit. Select Zone 1 and select AIR FRY. Then set the temperature to 350°F and set the time to 20 minutes. Select MATCH COOK to match the Settings in Zone 2 with those in Zone 1. Then select START/PAUSE to begin. 3. Once cooking has finished, serve as an appetizer.

Per Serving: Calories 12; Fat 1. 95g; Sodium 78mg; Carbs 2. 02g; Fiber 0. 9g; Sugar 0. 42g; Protein 1. 18g

---

Cheesy Tomato Bread

Prep Time: 10 minutes | Cook Time: 8 minutes | Serves: 4

1 friendly baguette
4 tsp. butter, melted
3 chopped garlic cloves

5 tsp. sundried tomato pesto
1 cup mozzarella cheese, grated

1. Cut the baguette into 5 thick round slices. 2. Add the garlic cloves to the melted butter and brush onto each slice of bread. 3. Spread a teaspoon of sun dried tomato pesto onto each slice. 4. Top each slice with the grated mozzarella. 5. Install the crisper plate in the basket, place the bread slices in the basket, and insert the basket into the unit. Select Zone 1 and select AIR FRY. Then set the temperature to 180°F and set the time to 8 minutes. Select START/PAUSE to begin. Cook them for 6 to 8 minutes. 6. Once cooking has finished, top with chili flakes, some freshly chopped basil leaves, and oregano if desired.

Per Serving: Calories 147; Fat 4. 49g; Sodium 378mg; Carbs 14. 82g; Fiber 2. 3g; Sugar 2. 38g; Protein 12. 32g

---

Sweet–Spicy Spare Ribs

Prep Time: 10 minutes | Cook Time: 35 minutes | Serves: 4

1½ pounds spare ribs
Kosher salt and ground black pepper, to taste
2 teaspoons brown sugar

1 teaspoon paprika
1 teaspoon chile powder
1 teaspoon garlic powder

1. Spray the crisper plate with olive oil. Toss all remaining ingredients. 2. Install the crisper plate in the basket, place the mixture in the basket, and insert the basket into the unit. 3. Select Zone 1 and select AIR FRY. Then set the temperature to 350°F and set the time to 35 minutes. Select START/PAUSE to begin. 4. Turn them over halfway through the cooking time. 5. Once cooking has finished, serve. Bon appétit!

Per Serving: Calories 254; Fat 9. 7g; Sodium 116mg; Carbs 3. 66g; Fiber 0. 5g; Sugar 1. 91g; Protein 35. 81g

Paprika Butter Roasted Carrots

Prep Time: 10 minutes | Cook Time: 15 minutes | Serves: 4

1 pound baby carrots
2 tablespoons butter
Kosher salt and ground white pepper, to taste

1 teaspoon paprika
1 teaspoon dried oregano

1. Toss the carrots with the remaining ingredients. 2. Install the crisper plate in the basket, place the carrots in the basket, and insert the basket into the unit. 3. Select Zone 1 and select AIR FRY. Then set the temperature to 380°F and set the time to 15 minutes. Select START/PAUSE to begin. 4. Shake the basket halfway through the cooking time. 5. Once cooking has finished, serve. Bon appétit!
Per Serving: Calories 97; Fat 6. 07g; Sodium 113mg; Carbs 10. 87g; Fiber 3. 9g; Sugar 4. 56g; Protein 1. 25g

Buttered Buffalo Cauliflower

Prep Time: 10 minutes | Cook Time: 15 minutes | Serves: 4

4 cups bite-sized cauliflower florets
1 cup friendly bread crumbs, mixed with 1 tsp. salt
¼ cup melted butter [vegan/other]

¼ cup buffalo sauce [vegan/other]
Mayo [vegan/other] or creamy dressing for dipping

1. In a bowl, combine the butter and buffalo sauce to create a creamy paste. 2. Completely cover each floret with the sauce. 3. Coat the florets with the bread crumb mixture. 4. Install the crisper plate in the basket, place the florets in the basket, and insert the basket into the unit. Select Zone 1 and select AIR FRY. Then set the temperature to 350°F and set the time to 15 minutes. Select START/PAUSE to begin. Shake the basket occasionally. 5. Once cooking has finished, serve with a raw vegetable salad, mayo or creamy dressing.
Per Serving: Calories 185; Fat 12. 4g; Sodium 360mg; Carbs 17. 03g; Fiber 2. 5g; Sugar 8. 56g; Protein 3. 12g

French Vermouth Mushrooms

Prep Time: 10 minutes | Cook Time: 27 minutes | Serves: 4

2 lb. button mushrooms
3 tbsp. white or French vermouth [optional]
1 tbsp. coconut oil

2 tsp. herbs of your choice
½ tsp. garlic powder

1. Wash and dry the mushrooms. Slice them into quarters. 2. Install the crisper plate in both baskets, place the coconut oil, garlic powder, and herbs in the baskets, and insert the baskets into the unit. Select Zone 1 and select AIR FRY. Then set the temperature to 320°F and set the time to 2 minutes. Select MATCH COOK to match the Settings in Zone 2 with those in Zone 1. Select START/PAUSE to begin. 3. Cook for 2 minutes and give a stir. Put the mushrooms in the basket to cook for 25 minutes and stir occasionally throughout. 4. Pour in the white vermouth and mix. Cook for another 5 minutes. 5. Once cooking has finished, serve hot.
Per Serving: Calories 86; Fat 4. 42g; Sodium 22mg; Carbs 8. 4g; Fiber 2. 4g; Sugar 4. 53g; Protein 7. 16g

Chapter 7 Dessert

90   Cheesy Orange Almond Fritters

90   Lemony Cheese Mini Pies

90   Cinnamon Peach Cake

91   Chocolate Coconut Bread Pudding

91   Coconut Strawberry Cake with Almond

91   Cinnamon Apple & Cranberry Dumplings

92   Vanilla Plum Dessert

92   Butter Chocolate Mini Cheesecakes

92   Sweet Cinnamon Chickpeas

93   Lemony Banana Beignets

93   Tasty Cinnamon Bananas

93   Sweet Raspberry Doughnuts

94   Healthy Fresh Fruit Crumble

94   Coconut Nuts Cookies

94   Lemony Strawberries

95   Whipped Cream Vanilla Cake

95   Yummy Chocolate Avocado

95   Vanilla Coconut Cream Pie

96   Vanilla Cocoa Bombs

96   Coconut Squash Pie

96   Cream Plum Delight

97   Butter Apple & Pecans Pie Bread Pudding

97   Buttered Raisin Bread Pudding

97   Mini Orange Raspberry Tarts

98   Chocolate Cream-Filled Mini Cakes

98   Lemony Coconut Poppy Seed Macaroons

99   Classic Little French Fudge Cakes

99   Sweet Chocolate Meringue Cookies

100   Delicious Halle Berries-and-Cream Cobbler

100   Creamy Peach & Almond Dessert

101   Lemony Curd Pavlova with Blueberries

101   Vanilla Chocolate Chip Cookies

Cheesy Orange Almond Fritters
Prep Time: 10 minutes | Cook Time: 4 minutes | Serves: 8

1½ tablespoons orange juice
½ teaspoon ground star anise
⅓ teaspoon ground cinnamon
2 tablespoons Truvia for baking
1¼ cups almond flour

1 teaspoon vanilla extract
¾ cup whole milk
1 teaspoon orange rind, grated
¾ lb. cream cheese, at room temperature

1. Combine all the ingredients in a bowl. 2. Install the crisper plate in the basket and place the teaspoons of the mixture in the basket. Insert the basket into the unit. Select Zone 1 and select AIR FRY. Then set the temperature to 340°F and set the time to 4 minutes. Select START/PAUSE to begin. 3. Once cooking has finished, serve.

Per Serving: Calories 166; Fat 12. 99g; Sodium 196mg; Carbs 8. 73g; Fiber 0. 1g; Sugar 6. 5g; Protein 3. 79g

Lemony Cheese Mini Pies
Prep Time: 10 minutes | Cook Time: 5 minutes | Serves: 8

1 box of lemon instant pudding
filling mix (4-serving size)
½ teaspoon ground star anise
⅛ teaspoon salt
1 teaspoon pure vanilla extract

1¼ cups cream cheese, room temperature
⅓ cup coconut, shredded
18 wonton wrappers
1 teaspoon lemon peel, grated

1. Spray muffin pan with olive oil cooking spray. Press the wonton wrappers evenly into cups. 2. Install the crisper plate in both baskets, place the cups in the baskets, and insert the baskets into the unit. Select Zone 1 and select BAKE. Then set the temperature to 350°F and set the time to 5 minutes. Select MATCH COOK to match the Settings in Zone 2 with those in Zone 1. Select START/PAUSE to begin. 3. Cook until the edges are golden. 4. Meanwhile, blend all remaining ingredients using blender. 5. Place the prepared cream in the fridge until ready to serve. Lastly, divide prepared cream among wrappers and keep refrigerated until ready to eat. 6. Once cooking has finished, serve.

Per Serving: Calories 413; Fat 11. 98g; Sodium 809mg; Carbs 66. 44g; Fiber 1. 9g; Sugar 7. 51g; Protein 9. 86g

Cinnamon Peach Cake
Prep Time: 10 minutes | Cook Time: 35 minutes | Serves: 6

½ lb. peaches, pitted and mashed
½ teaspoon baking powder
1¼ cups almond flour
½ teaspoon orange extract
¼ teaspoon nutmeg, freshly grated

2 eggs
2 tablespoons Truvia for baking
⅓ cup ghee
¼ teaspoon ground cinnamon
1 teaspoon pure vanilla extract

1. Spritz the cake pan with olive oil cooking spray. 2. In a mixing bowl, beat the ghee with Truvia until creamy. 3. Add the mashed peaches, egg, and honey. 4. Make the cake batter by mixing the remaining ingredients. 5. Stir in the peach mixture in with rest of ingredients. 6. Pour batter into cake pan and level the surface of batter. 7. Install the crisper plate in the basket, place the pan in the basket, and insert the basket into the unit. Select Zone 1 and select BAKE. Then set the temperature to 310°F and set the time to 35 minutes. Select START/PAUSE to begin. 8. Once cooking has finished, serve.

Per Serving: Calories 179; Fat 13. 58g; Sodium 24mg; Carbs 12. 98g; Fiber 0. 6g; Sugar 9. 52g; Protein 2. 08g

Chocolate Coconut Bread Pudding
Prep Time: 10 minutes | Cook Time: 35 minutes | Serves: 6

¾ cup chocolate chips
2 eggs plus 1 egg yolk, beaten
1 teaspoon candied ginger
3 ½ tablespoons coconut oil, room temperature
2 tablespoons Truvia for baking

⅓ cup coconut milk creamer
8 slices ciabatta bread, cubed
2 teaspoons rum
1 cup soy milk

1. Place cubed bread into bowl. 2. Combine remaining ingredients in another bowl and mix well. 3. Scrape the chocolate mix into first dish with bread cubes. Allow to soak for 20 minutes. 4. Evenly divide the mixture between 2 mini loaf pans. 5. Install the crisper plate in both baskets, place the pans in the baskets, and insert the baskets into the unit. Select Zone 1 and select BAKE. Then set the temperature to 305°F and set the time to 35 minutes. Select MATCH COOK to match the Settings in Zone 2 with those in Zone 1. Select START/PAUSE to begin. 6. Once cooking has finished, serve.
Per Serving: Calories 257; Fat 15. 98g; Sodium 200mg; Carbs 23. 42g; Fiber 1. 1g; Sugar 5. 03g; Protein 5. 06g

Coconut Strawberry Cake with Almond
Prep Time: 10 minutes | Cook Time: 17 minutes | Serves: 6

⅓ cup strawberry jam
⅓ cup almonds, slivered
3 eggs, beaten
1 stick butter
⅓ teaspoon baking powder
4-ounces coconut flour

1 tablespoon cornstarch (mix with flour)
½ teaspoon vanilla essence
⅓ teaspoon ground cinnamon
2 tablespoons Truvia for baking
1 teaspoon crystalized ginger
Olive oil cooking spray

1. Lightly grease the cake pan with olive oil cooking spray. 2. Whip the butter and Truvia using a blender. Add the almonds, eggs, and jam to beat again until well combined. 3. Add flour, vanilla essence, baking powder, ginger and ground cinnamon. 4. Install the crisper plate in the basket, place the pan in the basket, and insert the basket into the unit. Select Zone 1 and select BAKE. Then set the temperature to 310°F and set the time to 17 minutes. Select START/PAUSE to begin. 5. Once cooking has finished, serve.
Per Serving: Calories 233; Fat 20. 24g; Sodium 193mg; Carbs 8. 24g; Fiber 0. 5g; Sugar 3. 55g; Protein 4. 86g

Cinnamon Apple & Cranberry Dumplings
Prep Time: 10 minutes | Cook Time: 22 minutes | Serves: 4

1 teaspoon ground cinnamon
1 ½ tablespoons cranberries, dried
1 tablespoon butter, melted
4 Gala apples, cored and peeled

1 ½ sheets puff pastry
1 teaspoon ground cloves
1 ½ tablespoons Truvia for baking

1. Place each apple on one of the puff pastry sheets. 2. To make the filling, mix the dried cranberries, cinnamon, Truvia, and ground cloves. 3. Fill the apple cores with the cranberry mixture. Fold the puff pastry around the apples. Drizzle with melted butter. 4. Install the crisper plate in the basket, place the apple dumplings in the basket, and insert the basket into the unit. Select Zone 1 and select BAKE. Then set the temperature to 365°F and set the time to 22 minutes. Select START/PAUSE to begin. 5. Once cooking has finished, serve.
Per Serving: Calories 245; Fat 9. 99g; Sodium 70mg; Carbs 40. 18g; Fiber 5. 2g; Sugar 22. 34g; Protein 1. 85g

Vanilla Plum Dessert

Prep Time: 10 minutes | Cook Time: 35 minutes | Serves: 4

2 tablespoons Truvia for baking
1 teaspoon orange extract
¾ teaspoon candied ginger, minced
⅓ teaspoon ground cinnamon

2 tablespoons cornstarch
¾ lb. purple plums, pitted and halved
1 teaspoon vanilla essence

1. Spritz the cake pan with olive oil cooking spray. Add the plums to the bottom of pan. 2. Combine the remaining ingredients. Spread the mixture over the plum layer. 3. Install the crisper plate in the basket, place the pan in the basket, and insert the basket into the unit. Select Zone 1 and select BAKE. Then set the temperature to 380°F and set the time to 35 minutes. Select START/PAUSE to begin. 4. Once cooking has finished, serve.

Per Serving: Calories 124; Fat 0. 09g; Sodium 17mg; Carbs 31. 16g; Fiber 0. 9g; Sugar 22. 64g; Protein 0. 34g

Butter Chocolate Mini Cheesecakes

Prep Time: 10 minutes | Cook Time: 18 minutes | Serves: 8

For the crust:
⅓ teaspoon nutmeg, grated
1 tablespoon Truvia
½ cup graham cracker crumbs

1½ tablespoons melted butter
1 teaspoon ground cinnamon
A pinch of salt

For the Cheesecake:
2 eggs
1½ cups chocolate chips
1½ tablespoons sour cream

1 package soft cheese
2 tablespoons Truvia for baking
½ teaspoon vanilla essence

1. Firstly, line eight cups of mini muffin pan with paper liners. 2. To make the crust, mix the graham cracker crumbs together with 1 tablespoon Truvia, nutmeg, cinnamon, and salt. 3. Add the melted butter to moisten the crumb mixture. Divide the crumb mixture among the muffin cups and press gently to make even layers. 4. In another bowl, whip the sour cream, soft cheese, and 2 tablespoons Truvia until smooth. Add the eggs and vanilla essence in to the mix. Divide half of the chocolate chips among the prepared muffin cups. 5. Add the cheese mix to each muffin cup. Place another layer using remaining chocolate chips. 6. Install the crisper plate in both baskets, place the muffins in the baskets, and insert the baskets into the unit. Select Zone 1 and select BAKE. Then set the temperature to 345°F and set the time to 18 minutes. Select MATCH COOK to match the Settings in Zone 2 with those in Zone 1. Select START/PAUSE to begin. 7. Once cooking has finished, to finish, transfer mini cheesecakes to a cooling rake.

Per Serving: Calories 160; Fat 11. 12g; Sodium 459mg; Carbs 8. 56g; Fiber 0. 4g; Sugar 2. 15g; Protein 6. 7g

Sweet Cinnamon Chickpeas

Prep Time: 10 minutes | Cook Time: 10 minutes | Serves: 2

1 tbsp. sweetener
1 tbsp. cinnamon

1 C. chickpeas

1. Rinse and drain chickpeas. 2. Mix all ingredients together. 3. Install the crisper plate in the basket, put the chickpeas in the basket, and insert the basket into the unit. Select Zone 1 and select AIR FRY. Then set the temperature to 390°F and set the time to 10 minutes. Select START/PAUSE to begin. 4. Once cooking has finished, serve.

Per Serving: Calories 409; Fat 6. 12g; Sodium 25mg; Carbs 71. 36g; Fiber 14. 3g; Sugar 15. 48g; Protein 20. 63g

Lemony Banana Beignets
Prep Time: 10 minutes | Cook Time: 8 minutes | Serves: 6

1 cup almond flour
⅓ teaspoon nutmeg, freshly grated
½ teaspoon lemon juice
3 eggs
½ tablespoon baking powder
2 tablespoons Truvia for baking

1 teaspoon ground cloves
⅓ cup milk
1½ large-sized over-ripe bananas, peeled and sliced
½ teaspoon lemon peel, grated
A pinch of turmeric

1. In a bowl, drizzle banana slices with lemon juice. 2. In another bowl, combine the dry ingredients. 3. In second bowl, combine all the wet ingredients. 4. Place the wet mixture into the dry and combine well. Dip each banana slice into batter. 5. Install the crisper plate in both baskets, place the banana in the baskets, and insert the baskets into the unit. Select Zone 1 and select AIR FRY. Then set the temperature to 335°F and set the time to 8 minutes. Select MATCH COOK to match the Settings in Zone 2 with those in Zone 1. Select START/PAUSE to begin. 6. Once cooking has finished, serve.

Per Serving: Calories 95; Fat 2. 85g; Sodium 40mg; Carbs 14. 68g; Fiber 1. 2g; Sugar 7. 25g; Protein 3. 68g

Tasty Cinnamon Bananas
Prep Time: 5 minutes | Cook Time: 10 minutes | Serves: 2-3

1 C. panko breadcrumbs
3 tbsp. cinnamon
½ C. almond flour

3 egg whites
8 ripe bananas
3 tbsp. vegan coconut oil

1. Heat the coconut oil and add breadcrumbs. Mix around 2-3 minutes until golden. Pour into bowl. 2. Peel and cut the bananas in half. Roll each bananas half into the flour, eggs, and crumb mixture. 3. Install the crisper plate in both baskets, put the bananas in the baskets, and insert the baskets into the unit. Select Zone 1 and select AIR FRY. Then set the temperature to 280°F and set the time to 10 minutes. Select MATCH COOK to match the Settings in Zone 2 with those in Zone 1. Then select START/PAUSE to begin. 4. Once cooking has finished, serve.

Per Serving: Calories 577; Fat 16. 8g; Sodium 322mg; Carbs 104. 35g; Fiber 14g; Sugar 41. 13g; Protein 12. 19g

Sweet Raspberry Doughnuts
Prep Time: 10 minutes | Cook Time: 5 minutes | Serves: 8

1 package (16. 3 ounces) large refrigerator biscuits
Oil in mister

1¼ cups good-quality raspberry jam
Confectioners' sugar for dusting

1. Separate the biscuits into 8 rounds. Spray both sides of rounds lightly with oil. 2. Spray the crisper plates with oil. Install the crisper plate in both baskets, put the biscuits in the baskets, and insert the baskets into the unit. Select Zone 1 and select AIR FRY. Then set the temperature to 350°F and set the time to 5 minutes. Select MATCH COOK to match the Settings in Zone 2 with those in Zone 1. Then select START/PAUSE to begin. Cook until golden brown. 3. Once cooking has finished, transfer to a wire rack to let cool. 4. Fill a pastry bag, fitted with small plain tip, with raspberry jam. Use tip to poke a small hole in the side of each doughnut, then fill the centers with the jam. Dust doughnuts with confectioners' sugar.

Per Serving: Calories 62; Fat 1. 14g; Sodium 65mg; Carbs 12. 78g; Fiber 1. 5g; Sugar 8. 85g; Protein 0. 76g

Healthy Fresh Fruit Crumble
Prep Time: 10 minutes | Cook Time: 45 minutes | Serves: 5

1½ pounds baking apples (such as Gala) or firm-ripe pears
2 tablespoons brown sugar
½ teaspoon pie spice
1 teaspoon grated fresh ginger
2 teaspoons fresh lemon juice
½ cup all-purpose flour
Crumb Topping:

½ cup old-fashioned oats
¼ cup packed brown sugar
1 teaspoon finely grated lemon peel
¾ teaspoon apple pie spice
⅛ teaspoon salt
5 tablespoons butter, cut up
Vanilla ice cream or whipped cream, for topping

1. In a bowl, toss fruit with sugar, pie spice, ginger, and lemon juice. Install the crisper plate in the basket, put the hot fruit mixture in the basket, and insert the basket into the unit. Select Zone 1 and select AIR FRY. Then set the temperature to 375°F and set the time to 25 minutes. Select START/PAUSE to begin. Cook for 25 minutes, stirring twice. Press the fruit down with the back of a wooden spoon to compact. 2. Prepare the topping: Meanwhile, combine flour, oats, sugar, pie spice, lemon peel, and salt in a bowl. Blend in the butter until evenly crumbly. 3. Pull out the basket and spoon topping onto hot fruit mixture. 4. Reduce the temperature to 300°F. Cook for 20 minutes until golden and fruit is tender. 5. Once cooking has finished, serve with a scoop of vanilla ice cream or whipped cream.
Per Serving: Calories 348; Fat 14. 04g; Sodium 171mg; Carbs 58. 08g; Fiber 3. 2g; Sugar 37. 96g; Protein 4. 54g

Coconut Nuts Cookies
Prep Time: 15 minutes | Cook Time: 10 minutes | Serves: 6

½ cup butter, softened
1 cup coconut flour
3 oz macadamia nuts, grinded

½ teaspoon baking powder
3 tablespoons Erythritol
Cooking spray

1. In the mixing bowl, mix up the butter, coconut flour, baking powder, grinded coconut nuts, and Erythritol. 2. Knead the non-sticky dough. Cut the dough into small pieces and roll them into balls. Press every cookie ball gently to get the shape of cookies. 3. Spray the crisper plate with cooking spray. Install the crisper plate in both baskets, put the uncooked cookies in the baskets, and insert the baskets into the unit. Select Zone 1 and select AIR FRY. Then set the temperature to 365°F and set the time to 8 minutes. Select MATCH COOK to match the Settings in Zone 2 with those in Zone 1. Then select START/PAUSE to begin. 4. Then cook for extra 2 minutes at 390°F to get the light brown crust. 5. Once cooking has finished, serve.
Per Serving: Calories 265; Fat 26. 67g; Sodium 165mg; Carbs 7. 64g; Fiber 1. 7g; Sugar 5. 62g; Protein 1. 57g

Lemony Strawberries
Prep Time: 10 minutes | Cook Time: 20 minutes | Serves: 4

1 pound strawberries, halved
4 tablespoons stevia

1 tablespoon lemon juice
1 and ½ cups water

1. Install the crisper plate in the basket, put all the ingredients in the basket and toss, and insert the basket into the unit. 2. Select Zone 1 and select AIR FRY. Then set the temperature to 340°F and set the time to 20 minutes. Select START/PAUSE to begin. 3. Once cooking has finished, divide the stew into cups and serve cold.
Per Serving: Calories 76; Fat 0. 35g; Sodium 3mg; Carbs 18. 95g; Fiber 2. 3g; Sugar 15. 42g; Protein 0. 77g

Whipped Cream Vanilla Cake

Prep Time: 15 minutes | Cook Time: 25 minutes | Serves: 12

1 cup almond flour
½ cup coconut flour
¼ cup coconut oil, melted
3 eggs, beaten
1 teaspoon baking powder

1 teaspoon vanilla extract
1 teaspoon cream cheese
2 tablespoons Splenda
½ cup whipped cream

1. In the mixing bowl, mix up the coconut flour, almond flour, coconut oil, eggs, baking powder, vanilla extract, and cream cheese. Whisk the mixture well with the immersion blender. 2. Then line the crisper plate with baking paper. 3. Install the crisper plate in the basket, put the cake batter in the basket, and insert the basket into the unit. 4. Select Zone 1 and select AIR FRY. Then set the temperature to 355°F and set the time to 25 minutes. Select START/PAUSE to begin. 5. When cooking is up, cool the cake well. 6. Meanwhile, mix up the Splenda and whipped cream cheese. Spread the cake with whipped cream mixture. Serve.

Per Serving: Calories 79; Fat 7. 71g; Sodium 32mg; Carbs 1. 09g; Fiber 0. 1g; Sugar 0. 73g; Protein 1. 77g

Yummy Chocolate Avocado

Prep Time: 5 minutes | Cook Time: 20 minutes | Serves: 4

2 avocados, peeled, pitted and mashed
3 tablespoons chocolate, melted

4 tablespoons erythritol
3 tablespoons cream cheese, soft

1. Install the crisper plate in the basket, combine all the ingredients in the basket and whisk, and insert the basket into the unit. 2. Select Zone 1 and select AIR FRY. Then set the temperature to 340°F and set the time to 20 minutes. Select START/PAUSE to begin. 3. Once cooking has finished, divide into bowls and serve cold.

Per Serving: Calories 285; Fat 18. 28g; Sodium 77mg; Carbs 30. 5g; Fiber 7. 5g; Sugar 18. 02g; Protein 18. 28g

Vanilla Coconut Cream Pie

Prep Time: 15 minutes | Cook Time: 25 minutes | Serves: 4

4 tablespoons coconut cream
1 teaspoon baking powder
1 teaspoon apple cider vinegar
1 egg, beaten
¼ cup coconut flakes

1 teaspoon vanilla extract
½ cup coconut flour
4 teaspoons Splenda
1 teaspoon xanthan gum
Cooking spray

1. Put all liquid ingredients in the bowl: coconut cream, egg, apple cider vinegar, and vanilla extract. 2. Stir the liquid until homogenous and add baking powder, coconut flour, coconut flakes, Splenda, and xanthan gum. 3. Stir the ingredients until the smooth texture of the batter forms. 4. Spray the air fryer cake mold with cooking spray. Pour the batter in the cake mold. 5. Install the crisper plate in the basket, put the cake mold in the basket, and insert the basket into the unit. Select Zone 1 and select AIR FRY. Then set the temperature to 330°F and set the time to 25 minutes. Select START/PAUSE to begin. 6. Once cooking has finished, cool the cooked pie completely and remove it from the cake mold. Cut the cooked pie into servings. Serve.

Per Serving: Calories 123; Fat 9. 92g; Sodium 74mg; Carbs 5. 86g; Fiber 1. 2g; Sugar 3. 04g; Protein 3. 17g

Vanilla Cocoa Bombs

Prep Time: 5 minutes | Cook Time: 8 minutes | Serves: 12

2 cups macadamia nuts, chopped
4 tablespoons coconut oil, melted
1 teaspoon vanilla extract

¼ cup cocoa powder
⅓ cup swerve

1. In a bowl, mix all the ingredients and whisk well. Shape medium balls out of this mix. 2. Install the crisper plate in the basket, put the balls in the basket, and insert the basket into the unit. Select Zone 1 and select AIR FRY. Then set the temperature to 300°F and set the time to 8 minutes. Select START/PAUSE to begin. 3. Once cooking has finished, serve cold.

Per Serving: Calories 217; Fat 21. 69g; Sodium 2mg; Carbs 7. 47g; Fiber 2. 5g; Sugar 4. 32g; Protein 2. 09g

Coconut Squash Pie

Prep Time: 15 minutes | Cook Time: 35 minutes | Serves: 6

2 tablespoons Splenda
1 tablespoon Erythritol
5 eggs, beaten
4 tablespoons coconut flakes
¼ cup heavy cream

1 teaspoon vanilla extract
1 teaspoon butter
¼ teaspoon ground cinnamon
4 oz Kabocha squash, peeled

1. Grate the Kabocha squash. Then grease the baking mold with butter and put the grated Kabocha squash inside. 2. In the mixing bowl, mix up the Splenda, Erythritol, coconut flakes, vanilla extract, heavy cream, and ground cinnamon. Then pour the liquid over the Kabocha squash. Stir the mixture gently with the fork. 3. Install the crisper plate in the basket, put the mold with pie in the basket, and insert the basket into the unit. Select Zone 1 and select AIR FRY. Then set the temperature to 365°F and set the time to 35 minutes. Select START/PAUSE to begin. 4. Once cooking has finished, cool the cooked pie to the room temperature and cut into the servings. Serve.

Per Serving: Calories 162; Fat 11. 53g; Sodium 103mg; Carbs 6. 3g; Fiber 0. 7g; Sugar 3. 38g; Protein 7. 85g

Cream Plum Delight

Prep Time: 10 minutes | Cook Time: 18 minutes | Serves: 8

3 eggs
⅓ teaspoon pure hazelnut extract
2 tablespoons Truvia for baking
⅓ cup almond flour

A pinch of salt
1½ cups plums, pitted and halved
⅓ cup heavy cream

1. Firstly, butter 2 mini pie pans. Lay the plum halves on the bottoms of pans. 2. In a saucepan, over medium heat, warm the milk and heavy cream until well heated. Remove the pan from heat. Mix in the flour using a wire whisk. 3. In a bowl, whisk the eggs, with Truvia and salt until creamy. Whisk in the creamy milk mixture. Pour mixture over the plums. 4. Install the crisper plate in the basket, place the mixture in the basket, and insert the basket into the unit. Select Zone 1 and select BAKE. Then set the temperature to 335°F and set the time to 18 minutes. Select START/PAUSE to begin. 5. Once cooking has finished, serve.

Per Serving: Calories 124; Fat 5. 52g; Sodium 340mg; Carbs 15. 4g; Fiber 0. 4g; Sugar 12. 9g; Protein 3. 65g

Butter Apple & Pecans Pie Bread Pudding

Prep Time: 10 minutes | Cook Time: 28 minutes | Serves: 8

4 Granny Smith apples, peeled and chopped
2 large eggs, whisked
⅓ cup pecans, chopped
1 ⅓ cup milk
7 small-sized slices of sweet bread, torn into pieces

1 teaspoon apple pie spice
1½ tablespoons butter, softened
2 tablespoons cornstarch
2 tablespoons Truvia for baking

1. Take two mixing bowls. In the first bowl, add the bread pieces. In the second bowl, mix egg, milk, and apple pie spice. 2. Scrape milk/egg mixture into the first dish with sweet bread pieces. Allow to soak for 10 minutes and press with wide spatula. 3. Meanwhile, combine the Truvia, apples, and cornstarch. Place over the bread mixture. Drizzle melted butter over the top and top with chopped pecans. 4. Install the crisper plate in both baskets. Evenly divide the bread pudding mixture among 2 baskets. Insert the baskets into the unit. 5. Select Zone 1 and select BAKE. Then set the temperature to 315°F and set the time to 28 minutes. Select MATCH COOK to match the Settings in Zone 2 with those in Zone 1. Select START/PAUSE to begin. 6. Once cooking has finished, serve.

Per Serving: Calories 359; Fat 14. 13g; Sodium 163mg; Carbs 50. 68g; Fiber 4g; Sugar 18. 86g; Protein 7. 93g

Buttered Raisin Bread Pudding

Prep Time: 10 minutes | Cook Time: 28 minutes | Serves: 4

1 teaspoon cloves, ground
⅓ cup half-and-half
1 cup milk
4 slices sweet raisin bread, torn into pieces
1 tablespoon chocolate flavored liqueur

3 tablespoons butter, softened
1 teaspoon bergamot extract
⅓ teaspoon ground ginger
3 eggs lightly beaten
1 tablespoon Truvia for baking

1. In a bowl, add bread pieces. 2. In another bowl, add the remaining ingredients to mix well. 3. Scrape the mixture from second bowl, into bread bowl and let it soak for 15 minutes. Press with a wide spatula. 4. Install the crisper plate in both baskets. Evenly divide the bread pudding mixture among 2 baskets. Insert the baskets into the unit. 5. Select Zone 1 and select BAKE. Then set the temperature to 305°F and set the time to 28 minutes. Select MATCH COOK to match the Settings in Zone 2 with those in Zone 1. Select START/PAUSE to begin. 6. Once cooking has finished, serve.

Per Serving: Calories 251; Fat 14. 37g; Sodium 329mg; Carbs 22. 83g; Fiber 0. 8g; Sugar 17. 26g; Protein 7. 11g

Mini Orange Raspberry Tarts

Prep Time: 10 minutes | Cook Time: 10 minutes | Serves: 8

1½ tablespoons melted coconut oil
For the filling:
3 tablespoons orange juice
1 teaspoon ground cinnamon
1 teaspoon ground star anise
1½ tablespoons Truvia for baking

16 frozen tart shells, baked

2 cups fresh raspberries
1½ tablespoons cornstarch
1 teaspoon nutmeg, grated

1. To make the filling, cook all the filling ingredients over medium heat in a saucepan until raspberries burst and the juices have thickened. 2. Divide the filling among the tart shells with the melted coconut oil. 3. Install the crisper plate in both baskets, place the tart shells in the baskets, and insert the baskets into the unit. Select Zone 1 and select AIR FRY. Then set the temperature to 365°F and set the time to 10 minutes. Select MATCH COOK to match the Settings in Zone 2 with those in Zone 1. Select START/PAUSE to begin. 4. Once cooking has finished, serve.

Per Serving: Calories 226; Fat 8. 4g; Sodium 86mg; Carbs 36. 61g; Fiber 4. 1g; Sugar 15. 01g; Protein 2. 3g

Chocolate Cream–Filled Mini Cakes
Prep Time: 10 minutes | Cook Time: 10 minutes | Serves: 8

Cake:
½ cup (1 stick) unsalted butter (or coconut oil for dairy-free)
4 ounces unsweetened chocolate, chopped
Filing:
1 (8-ounce) package cream cheese (or Kite Hill brand cream cheese style spread for dairy-free), softened
For Garnish (Optional):
Whipped cream

¾ cup Swerve confectioners'-style sweetener or equivalent amount of powdered sweetener (see here)
3 large eggs

¼ cup Swerve confectioners'-style sweetener or equivalent amount of powdered or liquid sweetener (see here)

Raspberries

1. Grease the eight 4-ounce ramekins. 2. Make the cake batter: Heat the chocolate and butter in a saucepan over low heat and stir often until the chocolate is completely melted. Remove from the heat. 3. Add the sweetener and eggs and use a hand mixer on low to combine well. Set aside. 4. Make the cream filling: In a medium-sized bowl, mix together the cream cheese and sweetener until well combined. Taste and add more sweetener if desired. 5. Divide the chocolate mixture among the greased ramekins, filling each one halfway. Place 1 tablespoon of the filling on top of the chocolate mixture in each ramekin. 6. Install the crisper plate in both baskets, place the ramekins in the baskets, and insert the baskets into the unit. Select Zone 1 and select BAKE. Then set the temperature to 375°F and set the time to 10 minutes. Select MATCH COOK to match the Settings in Zone 2 with those in Zone 1. Select START/PAUSE to begin. Cook until the outside is set and the inside is soft and warm. 7. Once cooking has finished, allow to cool completely, then top with whipped cream, if desired, and garnish with raspberries, if desired. 8. Store without whipped cream in an airtight container in the refrigerator for up to 4 days or in the freezer for up to a month. Serve the leftovers chilled or reheat in a preheated 350°F air fryer for 5 minutes, or until heated through.
Per Serving: Calories 496; Fat 25. 83g; Sodium 265mg; Carbs 62. 89g; Fiber 1. 8g; Sugar 45. 98g; Protein 5. 47g

Lemony Coconut Poppy Seed Macaroons
Prep Time: 10 minutes | Cook Time: 14 minutes | Serves: 6

2 large egg whites, room temperature
⅓ cup Swerve confectioners'-style sweetener or equivalent amount of powdered sweetener (see here)
2 tablespoons grated lemon zest, plus more for garnish if desired
Lemon Icing:
¼ cup Swerve confectioners'-style sweetener or equivalent amount of powdered sweetener (see here)

2 teaspoons poppy seeds
1 teaspoon lemon extract
¼ teaspoon fine sea salt
2 cups unsweetened shredded coconut

1 tablespoon lemon juice

1. Line the crisper plate with parchment paper. 2. Place the egg whites in a medium-sized bowl and use a hand mixer on high to beat the whites until stiff peaks form. Add the sweetener, poppy seeds, lemon extract, lemon zest, and salt. Mix on low until combined. Gently fold in the coconut with a rubber spatula. 3. Use a 1-inch cookie scoop to place the cookies on the parchment, spacing them about ¼ inch apart. Install the crisper plate in both baskets, place the cookies in the baskets, and insert the baskets into the unit. Select Zone 1 and select BAKE. Then set the temperature to 325°F and set the time to 14 minutes. Select MATCH COOK to match the Settings in Zone 2 with those in Zone 1. Select START/PAUSE to begin. Cook until the cookies are golden and a toothpick inserted into the center comes out clean. 4. While the cookies bake, make the lemon icing: Place the sweetener in a small bowl. Add the lemon juice to stir well. If the icing is too thin, add a little more sweetener. If the icing is too thick, add a little more lemon juice. 5. Once cooking has finished, remove the cookies and allow to cool for about 10 minutes, then drizzle with the icing. Garnish with lemon zest, if desired. 6. Place the leftovers in an airtight container and store in the fridge for 5 days or in the freezer for a month.
Per Serving: Calories 97; Fat 0. 59g; Sodium 202mg; Carbs 22. 85g; Fiber 1. 1g; Sugar 19. 97g; Protein 1. 97g

Classic Little French Fudge Cakes

Prep Time: 10 minutes | Cook Time: 25 minutes | Serves: 12

Cakes:

3 cups blanched almond flour

¾ cup unsweetened cocoa powder

1 teaspoon baking soda

½ teaspoon fine sea salt

6 large eggs

1 cup Swerve confectioners'-style sweetener or equivalent amount of powdered sweetener (see here)

1½ cups canned pumpkin puree

3 tablespoons brewed decaf espresso or other strong brewed decaf coffee

3 tablespoons unsalted butter, melted but not hot (or coconut oil for dairy-free)

1 teaspoon vanilla extract

Cream Cheese Frosting:

½ cup Swerve confectioners'-style sweetener or equivalent amount of powdered or liquid sweetener (see here)

½ cup (1 stick) unsalted butter, melted (or coconut oil for dairy-free)

4 ounces cream cheese (½ cup) (or Kite Hill brand cream cheese style spread for dairy-free), softened

3 tablespoons unsweetened, unflavored almond milk or heavy cream

Chocolate Drizzle:

3 tablespoons unsalted butter, melted (or coconut oil for dairy-free)

2 tablespoons Swerve confectioners'-style sweetener or equivalent amount of powdered or liquid sweetener (see

here)

2 tablespoons unsweetened cocoa powder

¼ cup unsweetened, unflavored almond milk

½ cup chopped walnuts or pecans, for garnish (optional)

1. Spray the crisper plates with coconut oil. 2. Whisk together the flour, cocoa powder, baking soda, and salt in a medium-sized bowl until blended. 3. In a large bowl, beat the eggs and sweetener with a hand mixer for 2 to 3 minutes until light and fluffy. Add the pumpkin puree, melted butter, espresso, and vanilla and stir to combine. 4. Add the wet ingredients to the dry ingredients and stir until just combined. 5. Install the crisper plate in both baskets, place the batter in the baskets, filling each well two-thirds full, and insert the baskets into the unit. Select Zone 1 and select BAKE. Then set the temperature to 350°F and set the time to 25 minutes. Select MATCH COOK to match the Settings in Zone 2 with those in Zone 1. Select START/PAUSE to begin. Cook until a toothpick inserted into the center of a cake comes out clean. 6. Once cooking has finished, allow the cakes to cool completely in the basket before removing them. 7. Make the frosting: In a large bowl, mix the melted butter, sweetener, and cream cheese until well combined. Place in the almond milk and stir to combine. 8. Make the chocolate drizzle: Stir together the sweetener, melted butter, and cocoa powder in a small bowl until well combined. Add the almond milk while stirring to thin the mixture. 9. After the cakes have cooled, dip the tops of the cakes into the frosting, then use a spoon to drizzle the chocolate over each frosted cake. If desired, garnish the cakes with chopped nuts. 10. Store the leftovers in an airtight container in the refrigerator for up to 4 days or in the freezer for up to a month.

Per Serving: Calories 368; Fat 17. 64g; Sodium 362mg; Carbs 51. 98g; Fiber 3. 4g; Sugar 36. 74g; Protein 6. 19g

Sweet Chocolate Meringue Cookies

Prep Time: 10 minutes | Cook Time: 60 minutes | Serves: 8

3 large egg whites

¼ teaspoon cream of tartar

¼ cup Swerve confectioners'-style sweetener or equivalent

amount of powdered sweetener (see here)

2 tablespoons unsweetened cocoa powder

1. Line the crisper plate with parchment paper. 2. In a small bowl, use a hand mixer to beat the cream of tartar and egg whites until soft peaks form. With the mixer on low, slowly sprinkle in the sweetener and mix until it's completely incorporated. Continue to beat with the mixer until stiff peaks form. 3. Add the cocoa powder and gently fold until it's completely combined. 4. Spoon the mixture into a piping bag with a ¾-inch tip. Pipe sixteen 1-inch meringue cookies onto the lined pie pan, spacing them about ¼ inch apart. 5. Install the crisper plate in the basket, place the cookies in the basket, and insert the basket into the unit. Select Zone 1 and select BAKE. Then set the temperature to 225°F and set the time to 60 minutes. Select START/PAUSE to begin. 6. Cook until the cookies are crispy on the outside. 7. Once cooking has finished, let the cookies stand in the basket for another 20 minutes before removing and serving.

Per Serving: Calories 32; Fat 0. 2g; Sodium 22mg; Carbs 7. 06g; Fiber 0. 4g; Sugar 5. 79g; Protein 1. 59g

Delicious Halle Berries–and–Cream Cobbler

Prep Time: 10 minutes | Cook Time: 25 minutes | Serves: 4

12 ounces cream cheese (1½ cups), softened
1 large egg
¾ cup Swerve confectioners'-style sweetener or equivalent amount of powdered sweetener (see here)
Biscuits:
3 large egg whites
¾ cup blanched almond flour
1 teaspoon baking powder
Frosting:
2 ounces cream cheese (¼ cup), softened
1 tablespoon Swerve confectioners'-style sweetener or equivalent amount of powdered or liquid sweetener (see here)

½ teaspoon vanilla extract
¼ teaspoon fine sea salt
1 cup sliced fresh raspberries or strawberries

2½ tablespoons very cold unsalted butter, cut into pieces (see Tip)
¼ teaspoon fine sea salt

1 tablespoon unsweetened, unflavored almond milk or heavy cream
Fresh raspberries or strawberries, for garnish

1. Grease the crisper plate. 2. In a large mixing bowl, use a hand mixer to combine the egg, cream cheese, and sweetener until smooth. Stir in the vanilla and salt. Gently add the raspberries with a rubber spatula. Pour the mixture into the basket and set aside. 3. Make the biscuits: Place the egg whites in a medium-sized mixing bowl or the bowl of a stand mixer. Whip the egg whites until very fluffy and stiff with a hand mixer or stand mixer. 4. In a separate medium-sized bowl, combine the almond flour with baking powder. Cut in the butter and add the salt, stirring gently to keep the butter pieces intact. 5. Gently fold the almond flour mixture into the egg whites. Scoop out the dough and form it into a 2-inch-wide biscuit with a large spoon or ice cream scooper, making sure the butter stays in separate clumps. Place the biscuit on top of the raspberry mixture in the basket. Repeat with remaining dough to make 4 biscuits. 6. Install the crisper plate in both baskets, place the biscuits in the baskets, and insert the baskets into the unit. Select Zone 1 and select BAKE. Then set the temperature to 400°F and set the time to 5 minutes. Select MATCH COOK to match the Settings in Zone 2 with those in Zone 1. Select START/PAUSE to begin. Lower the temperature to 325°F and bake for another 17 to 20 minutes, until the biscuits are golden brown. 7. While the cobbler cooks, make the frosting: Place the cream cheese in a small bowl and stir to break it up. Add the sweetener to stir. Add the almond milk to stir until well combined. If you prefer a thinner frosting, add more almond milk. 8. Once cooking has finished, remove the cobbler and allow to cool slightly, then drizzle with the frosting. Garnish with fresh raspberries. 9. Store the leftovers in an airtight container in the refrigerator for up to 3 days. Reheat the cobbler in a preheated 350°F air fryer for 3 minutes, or until warmed through.
Per Serving: Calories 636; Fat 37. 23g; Sodium 833mg; Carbs 66. 26g; Fiber 2. 7g; Sugar 42. 43g; Protein 13. 31g

Creamy Peach & Almond Dessert

Prep Time: 10 minutes | Cook Time: 38 minutes | Serves: 6

6 peaches, pitted and halved
⅓ almonds, chopped
Well-chilled heavy cream to serve
1 teaspoon pure vanilla extract

Coconut oil spray for pan
2 tablespoons Truvia for baking
1 teaspoon candied ginger

1. Firstly, spray the crisper plate with coconut oil spray. 2. Install the crisper plate in the basket, place the peaches in the basket, and insert the basket into the unit. 3. In a bowl, combine almonds, vanilla, Truvia, candied ginger. Scrape this mixture into the basket over the peaches. 4. Select Zone 1 and select BAKE. Then set the temperature to 380°F and set the time to 38 minutes. Select START/PAUSE to begin. 5. Once cooking has finished, garnish dessert with heavy cream.
Per Serving: Calories 193; Fat 2. 24g; Sodium 20mg; Carbs 45. 9g; Fiber 2. 6g; Sugar 39. 61g; Protein 1. 31g

Lemony Curd Pavlova with Blueberries

Prep Time: 10 minutes | Cook Time: 60 minutes | Serves: 4

Shell:
3 large egg whites
¼ teaspoon cream of tartar
¾ cup Swerve confectioners'-style sweetener or equivalent

amount of powdered sweetener (see here)
1 teaspoon grated lemon zest
1 teaspoon lemon extract

Lemon Curd:
1 cup Swerve confectioners'-style sweetener or equivalent
amount of liquid or powdered sweetener (see here)
½ cup lemon juice

4 large eggs
½ cup coconut oil

For Garnish (Optional):
Blueberries
Swerve confectioners'-style sweetener or equivalent

amount of powdered sweetener (see here)

1. Thoroughly grease the crisper plate with butter or coconut oil. 2. Make the shell: In a small bowl, use a hand mixer to beat the cream of tartar and egg whites until soft peaks form. With the mixer on low, slowly sprinkle in the sweetener and mix until it's completely incorporated. 3. Add the lemon extract and lemon zest and continue to beat with the hand mixer until stiff peaks form. 4. Install the crisper plate in both baskets, spoon the mixture into the baskets, then smooth it across the bottom, up the sides, and onto the rim to form a shell. Insert the baskets into the unit. Select Zone 1 and select BAKE. Then set the temperature to 275°F and set the time to 60 minutes. Select MATCH COOK to match the Settings in Zone 2 with those in Zone 1. Select START/PAUSE to begin. Once cooking has finished, let the shell stand in the basket for 20 minutes. 5. While the shell bakes, make the lemon curd: In a medium-sized heavy-bottomed saucepan, whisk together the lemon juice, sweetener, and eggs. Add the coconut oil and place the pan on the stovetop over medium heat. Once the oil is melted, whisk constantly until the mixture thickens, thickly coating the back of a spoon, about 10 minutes. Do not allow the mixture to come to a boil. 6. Pour the lemon curd mixture through a fine-mesh strainer into a medium-sized bowl. Place the bowl inside a larger bowl filled with ice water and whisk occasionally until completely cool, about 15 minutes. 7. Place the lemon curd on top of the shell and garnish with blueberries and powdered sweetener, if desired. Store the leftovers in the refrigerator for up to 4 days.
Per Serving: Calories 480; Fat 32. 12g; Sodium 267mg; Carbs 48. 35g; Fiber 1. 8g; Sugar 39. 83g; Protein 6. 26g

Vanilla Chocolate Chip Cookies

Prep Time: 10 minutes | Cook Time: 15 minutes | Serves: 6

2 cups almond flour
¼ cup Swerve sugar replacement
Scant ½ teaspoon salt
¼ teaspoon baking soda
½ cup sugar-free chocolate chips

½ cup chopped pecans
¼ cup coconut oil
1 teaspoon vanilla extract
2 tablespoons milk, as needed

1. Line the basket with parchment paper. 2. Combine the almond flour, Swerve, baking soda, chocolate chips, salt, and pecans in a large bowl. Add the vanilla extract and coconut oil to stir until thoroughly combined. Add the milk, a teaspoon or two at a time as needed, until the mixture forms a stiff dough. 3. Roll the dough into 12 equal-size balls. Flatten slightly to form cookie-shaped disks. Install the crisper plate in both baskets, place the cookies in the baskets, and insert the baskets into the unit. Select Zone 1 and select BAKE. Then set the temperature to 300°F and set the time to 10 minutes. Select MATCH COOK to match the Settings in Zone 2 with those in Zone 1. Select START/PAUSE to begin. 4. Cook until the cookies begin to brown. 5. Once cooking has finished, cool completely before removing from the basket (the cookies will harden as they cool).
Per Serving: Calories 182; Fat 16. 73g; Sodium 271mg; Carbs 8. 89g; Fiber 1. 1g; Sugar 4. 82g; Protein 1. 28g

The Ninja is a superbly constructed air fryer that has the unusual ability to simultaneously cook two different dishes at different temperatures. This air fryer is excellent for feeding a family, whether everyone will eat the same thing or you need to prepare two separate dishes to suit everyone's preferences. Each basket can accommodate a pound of food. There is a small learning curve at first, but once you get the programming down, it's simple to use. With the exception of homemade fries, it will fry most things you throw into it without difficulty and quickly because there is no requirement for preheating.

Appendix 1 Measurement Conversion Chart

VOLUME EQUIVALENTS (LIQUID)

US STANDARD	US STANDARD (OUNCES)	METRIC (APPROXIMATE)
2 tablespoons	1 fl.oz	30 mL
¼ cup	2 fl.oz	60 mL
½ cup	4 fl.oz	120 mL
1 cup	8 fl.oz	240 mL
1½ cup	12 fl.oz	355 mL
2 cups or 1 pint	16 fl.oz	475 mL
4 cups or 1 quart	32 fl.oz	1 L
1 gallon	128 fl.oz	4 L

VOLUME EQUIVALENTS (DRY)

US STANDARD	METRIC (APPROXIMATE)
⅛ teaspoon	0.5 mL
¼ teaspoon	1 mL
½ teaspoon	2 mL
¾ teaspoon	4 mL
1 teaspoon	5 mL
1 tablespoon	15 mL
¼ cup	59 mL
½ cup	118 mL
¾ cup	177 mL
1 cup	235 mL
2 cups	475 mL
3 cups	700 mL
4 cups	1 L

TEMPERATURES EQUIVALENTS

FAHRENHEIT(F)	CELSIUS(C) (APPROXIMATE)
225 °F	107 °C
250 °F	120 °C
275 °F	135 °C
300 °F	150 °C
325 °F	160 °C
350 °F	180 °C
375 °F	190 °C
400 °F	205 °C
425 °F	220 °C
450 °F	235 °C
475 °F	245 °C
500 °F	260 °C

WEIGHT EQUIVALENTS

US STANDARD	METRIC (APPROXINATE)
1 ounce	28 g
2 ounces	57 g
5 ounces	142 g
10 ounces	284 g
15 ounces	425 g
16 ounces (1 pound)	455 g
1.5 pounds	680 g
2 pounds	907 g

Appendix 2 Air Fryer Cooking Chart

Vegetables	Temp(°F)	Time
Asparagus (1" slices)	400	5
Beets (whole)	400	40
Broccoli Florets	400	6
Brussel Sprouts (halved)	380	12-15
Carrots (1/2" slices)	360	12-15
Cauliflower Florets	400	10-12
Corn on the Cob	390	6-7
Eggplant (1 1/2" cubes)	400	12-15
Green Beans	400	4-6
Kale Leaves	250	12
Mushrooms (1/4" slices)	400	4-5
Onions (pearl)	400	10
Peppers (1" chunks)	380	8-15
Potatoes (whole)	400	30-40
Potatoes (wedges)	390	15-18
Potatoes (1" cubes)	390	12-15
Potatoes (baby, 1.5 lbs.)	400	15
Squash (1" cubes)	390	15
Sweet Potato (whole)	380	30-35
Tomatoes (cherry)	400	5
Zucchini (1/2" sticks)	400	10-12

Frozen Foods	Temp(°F)	Time
Breaded Shrimp	400	8-9
Chicken Burger	360	12
Chicken Nuggets	370	10-12
Chicken Strips	380	12-15
Corn Dogs	400	7-9
Fish Fillets (1-2 lbs.)	400	10-12
Fish Sticks	390	12-15
French Fries	380	12-17
Hash Brown Patties	380	10-12
Meatballs (1-inch)	350	10-12
Mozzarella Sticks (11 oz.)	400	8
Meat Pies (1-2 pies)	370	23-25
Mozzarella Sticks	390	7-9
Onion Rings	400	10-12
Pizza	390	5-10
Tater Tots	380	15-17

Beef	Temp(°F)	Time (r
Burgers (1/4 Pound)	350	8-1
Filet Mignon (4 oz.)	370	15-2
Flank Steak (1.5 lbs)	400	10-1
Meatballs (1 inch)	380	7-1(
London Broil (2.5 lbs.)	400	22-2
Round Roast (4 lbs)	390	45-5
Sirloin Steak (12oz)	390	9-1∙

Fish & Seafood	Temp(°F)	Tim
Calamari	400	4-5
Fish Fillets	400	10-1
Salmon Fillets	350	8-12
Scallops	400	5-7
Shrimp	370	5-7
Lobster Tails	370	5-7
Tuna Steaks	400	7-1(

Chicken	Temp(°F)	Time(n
Chicken Whole (3.5 lbs)	350	45-6∙
Chicken Breast (boneless)	380	12-1
Chicken Breast (bone-in)	350	22-2.
Chicken Drumsticks	380	23-2:
Chicken Thighs (bone-in)	380	23-2.
Chicken Tenders	350	8-12
Chicken Wings	380	22-2.

Pork & Lamb	Temp(°F)	Tim
Bacon	350	8-1:
Lamb Chops	400	8-12
Pork Chops (1" boneless)	400	8-10
Pork Loin (2 lbs.)	360	18-2
Rack of Lamb (24-32 oz.)	375	22-2:
Ribs	400	10-1:
Sausages	380	10-1:

Appendix 3 Recipes Index

Made in the USA
Las Vegas, NV
08 December 2024

13597526R00065